How I got Published

And What I Learned Along the Way

Edited by Lyn Worthen
and Renee Scandalis

Camden Park Press

How I Got Published
And What I Learned Along the Way

Table of Contents

Foreword

Renee Scandalis

There are all types of writers, those that "burned the boats" to write exclusively and those writing in their spare time; those who knew they wanted to write from the moment they first held a pencil to those who made the career choice later in life; those with a master's in creative writing and those with no formal training.

Whatever their journey, most writers want desperately to see their art recognized by publication, but the road to discovery is often a crooked, seemingly hidden path. A lonely profession to begin with, when starting out, one may feel as if they need a machete and a prayer to hack their way through. And where does one start?

How I Got Published and What I Learned Along the Way is a collection of firsthand accounts and advice from authors answering this question in their own unique style while seeking to give the burgeoning writer a Brush Hog to clear the way.

These essays cover a wide range of writing experience, from authors recently published for the first time to seasoned writers with decades of experience and dozens of publishing credits. They also cover the many different avenues to publication, from traditional to emerging markets, with insights and ideas to try and pitfalls to avoid.

Within these pages you will find contributions from authors of fiction and nonfiction, novels and short works, those that were traditionally published, and those that have self-published with success. There are stories of novelists and sports columnists, short-story writers and bloggers. Each author has taken a different career path. They all approach writing differently – and there is something here for everyone.

If you're reading this, then you are one of the few willing to spend time learning new things and improving yourself. The idea for this book came during just such an endeavor. At the Landmark Worldwide's Self-Expression and Leadership course, participants were challenged to create a project in a community that was important to us, to get members of the community to participate in the project, to find someone who would take over the leadership of the project.

I am so grateful to the many writers who gave me advice as the concept and the proposal were coming together. I am grateful to the writers who have contributed their wisdom in these pages. And I am grateful to Lyn Worthen for taking on the leadership role and to Camden Park Press for agreeing to publish the book. One of the goals of the Landmark program is to make a difference in the world, and many worthwhile and long lasting public works have been created through SELP. In the spirit of giving back, a portion of the proceeds will be donated to Children's Literacy Initiative. Thank you for helping to make a difference through your purchase.

We hope this book will inspire you to get your writing published and that you learn something along the way.

Enjoy the journey!

Renee Scandalis
Providence Village, TX
September 7, 2019

Introduction: Roller-Skating, Backwards, in the Rain

Lyn Worthen

In nearly every profession, aspirants spend months, if not years, learning the tricks and tools of the trade before ever being allowed to fly solo. Dancers, gymnasts, and figure-skaters begin their training at an early age, developing the muscle memory required for their art. Doctors, software developers, and welders go through extensive educational programs before entering their field.

But beyond the rudimentary basics of spelling and grammar, writers are left almost entirely to their own devices to figure out the ins and outs of what the general public considers a solitary, artistic pursuit at best and little more than a hobby at worst – when, in reality, writing is the foundation for much of the entertainment industry.

There's a lot to learn.

One way to illustrate the writing profession is through a metaphor:

Roller-skating = *Learn the craft*
Backwards = *Learn the business*
In the Rain = *Learn to get out of your own way*

Let me elaborate.

If you've ever tried to roller-skate, then you already know that learning the craft of writing is like learning to skate.

We fall on our butts a lot. But there are beginning writers who, through sheer determination, keep getting back up, dusting ourselves off and applying bandages to scraped knees and bruised egos where needed. And then we try again.

It's easier when there's someone around to pack us in padding and help us learn to keep our balance as we learn how to take the worlds and characters and stories in our heads and put them on the page in a way that will make sense to a reader.

I was fortunate in connecting with other writers as a teenager – though I had second thoughts after being told by my first mentor (an established author in children's fiction) that my writing was better suited to adults, and she really couldn't help me. At the time, I thought "writing adult fiction" meant including lots of sex, violence, and swearing in my stories, and I didn't know how to write any of those without it all sounding silly.

But she was encouraging, and promised me the resources were out there, so I kept searching, gradually scraping together my own "how to write" curriculum.

Back in those days, I would have viewed a book like this one as a handhold on that skating rink, reminding me that I wasn't pursuing this whole writing thing on my own; that others had skated on similar bumpy roads and worn a path that, while not entirely bump-free, was definitely much easier to travel.

*

As I got better at the craft, I discovered countless new worlds. Opportunities to pursue non-fiction and a career in editing, both of which I appeared to have a knack for, lured me away from writing fiction.

Challenges to write in new-to-me genres drew me back.

My fellow "skaters" urged caution, but never one to do only one thing when three more were beckoning simultaneously, I dove in headfirst, drawing on all the resources so freely shared by my writing colleagues.

Breaking into indie publishing and learning about contracts and copyrights and royalties and more was the writerly equivalent of learning to skate backwards. Writing to deadline and to special editorial requests taught me to skate in formation. And when I began building multi-author anthologies, it was not unlike learning to do the occasional literary backflip.

In other words, I learned the *business* of publishing.

*

While it's not an exaggeration to say that writers live in their heads (more accurately, in the worlds they've created in their heads), even the most introverted can benefit from being part of a community of like-minded craftspeople. I've never met a group of professionals who are more willing to share what they've learned with both newcomers to the profession and those who are rising in the ranks.

This is where this book comes in.

In these pages, twenty authors at various stages in their careers – from their first publications to seasoned professionals – share their stories. Some of them have worked their way through traditional publishing. Some have made their mark in indie publishing. And several are hybrid, with a foot planted solidly in each camp.

And while you will see similarities and parallels in their stories, you will also find differences. Some of these writers began at an early age, others later in life. They came to writing from a variety of career fields, and have chosen to write in different forms and genres.

They've worked through extreme highs and deep depression. They've juggled work and family and health challenges. And they brought their lessons to the page to let you know that when the stormclouds gather, you're not alone. Like so many others, you can reach inside and find what it takes to get past the challenges. You can learn how to get out of your own way.

You can learn to roller-skate backwards, in the rain.

Read their stories. Learn from them. Take guidance and inspiration and encouragement from their journeys – and know that your own path will be as unique to you as theirs are. Because there is no "one right way" to be a writer.

No single path every career must follow.

Write from your heart. Write from your passion. Write because it brings you joy or helps you purge your pain. Write because you can't *not* write.

We're looking forward to reading what you create.

– Lyn Worthen
Sandy, Utah
September 21, 2019

How I Got Published

And What I Learned Along the Way

The Power of Yes
Maxwell Alexander Drake

"How did you first get published?"

Above all other questions I get asked as I travel around the world teaching writing and promoting the projects I write for, that question is the one I hate the most. Why? Because no one likes my answer.

The truth is, I've never been rejected.

Yes, I get that I've been a fulltime professional writer for about fifteen years now, with a resume that's not too shabby. And yes, I get that every other professional writer has their story of how they were rejected hundreds of times before they finally convinced someone to give them their first break. Still, facts are facts. I've never been rejected. That may sound like a brag, but it's not.

I've never been rejected because I've never officially submitted anything. Ever.

Before you get all, "Well, us normal mortals can't get that lucky and have careers built from rainbows served on silver platters!" let me take you on a journey. One that will hopefully end with a small piece of wisdom or two you can use to help build your own professional writing career.

But instead of starting at the beginning, let's start at the end.

Last year I sold not one, but *two* movie scripts. The crazy thing is, *BOTH* were sold before I even wrote the first word of either script. If you know the movie industry at all, you know that never happens. You must write a script first, *THEN* you can sell it. Still, my bank account will confirm that I was paid quite handsomely before I ever wrote the first word of either of those movie scripts.

Even more insane is when you learn that I really wasn't a movie script writer when I sold them. I had, however, been studying *how* movie scripts were written. All mediums of writing are fascinating for me, and for about two years I had been learning all I could about writing movie scripts.

So, when the call came in from some random producer I'd never met and he said, "I love how you write and craft stories. I'm a movie producer. Can you write movie scripts?" I was able to honestly answer, "Yes. Yes, I can."

At this point you should be asking, "How did you get some random movie producer to just call you up and pay you to write movie scripts?" Well, that random movie producer reached out to me because he was a huge fan of the stories I wrote for Sony's *EverQuest Next*.

Did I mention I was the Lead Fiction Writer for a six-hundred-and-fifty-million-dollar video game from Sony? Yup. That was me. The thing is, before I worked for Sony, I didn't know the first thing about writing for video games.

So how the hell did I get hired to be the Lead Fiction Writer for the next installment of the *EverQuest* franchise – Sony Online Entertainment's flagship online roleplaying game?

Sony asked me to do it.

Yup. Sony approached me and, after making me sign a very scarily worded NDA, said how much they liked how I wrote and crafted stories, and offered me the Lead Writer job.

Now, as I said, to that point I'd never worked in the video game market. Hell, outside of playing a ton of games, I honestly knew nothing about the industry at all.

Still, when Sony asked me if I could do it, I said, "Yes. Yes, I can."

"But, wait!" You're probably thinking. "How did you catch the attention of a multi-billion-dollar entertainment company?"

Because they were fans of my novels, of course. But to understand how they became fans of my novels we must take another step back.

You see, I teach writing all over the world. I also hold the distinction of being the only writer to have taught writing classes at

San Diego Comic Con every year for the past ten years. And back in 2010ish, the people in charge of the *EverQuest* franchise started coming to my classes there in San Diego. They liked what I had to say enough to hire me to come in and teach the entire Sony Online Entertainment staff. They also purchased a bunch of my novels for the office. And those who read them fell in love with the stories I created.

Yet this doesn't answer the question, "How did you get the chance to teach writing classes at the largest fan convention in the U.S.?"

Taking another step back, I created my writing classes because when I was attending writers' conferences back before I was a published writer, I was never satisfied with the classes that were given. Many either had information that was so obvious as to be insulting, or worse, they were a fifty-five-minute session of, "Buy my book!"

I vowed that if I ever got the chance to teach classes like that, I'd *never* make those mistakes.

So, I created a few classes and started asking conventions if they wanted me to present for them. Back then, San Diego Comic Con was just starting its "How To" program. Since it was new, and they were looking to fill the slots, they gave me a shot.

They let me give *one* class. That class was so popular that Comic Con received more emails about me than any other single thing that year.

Because of this, they invited me back and let me teach four classes the following year. Those classes were so popular that Comic Con received more emails about me than about the rest of the entire convention combined!

So, because I put so much effort into making my writing classes as information-packed as I could, attendees loved them. I put time and effort into making the best product possible.

But why was I even at San Diego Comic Con in the first place? Even back in 2008 there was about an eight-year waiting list to get in as an exhibitor. Well, when my first little fantasy book was published, a vender who was going to be at Comic Con asked me if I would be a guest in his booth. He had read my book and was a huge fan of my writing and how I crafted stories.

I, of course, said, "Yes. Yes, I can."

And that finally brings us back to original question – "How did I get published in the first place?"

Well, this was in the early two-thousands. And while the Internet existed, it wasn't the Internet of today. Sure, there were websites, ecommerce, etc. But it wasn't the everyday tool that it is today.

I was, however, a very early adopter of the technology. In fact, the life I led before becoming a writer was that of an I.T. professional. So, since I had the knowledge, when I started writing I put up an Author's Page.

Sure, I get that today having an Author's Page is just something you must do. But back in 2006, authors didn't have websites. Not many, anyway.

But I did.

What was I using my website for? Well, I was writing what would become the ninth novel I ever wrote. And as I wrote it, I was posting pages for free on my website. To be honest, I was really just hoping someone, *anyone*, would read it.

And someone *did* read it. A man by the name of Patrick LoBrutto. (If you don't know the name, it's O.K. He's an editor. No one really knows editors. Still, he was the first editor for Raymond Feist, and has also edited for authors like Stephen King, Isaac Asimov, and the Louis L'Amour foundation.) Patrick was coming to Las Vegas to be a guest at a local writers' conference. And since it was odd for a writer to have their own website back then, especially an unpublished writer, he decided to check mine out. And you know what he discovered when he read the novel I was throwing up for free? He discovered that he really liked the way I wrote and how I crafted stories.

So, before the conference he called me up, told me who he was, and asked if I could have dinner with him the night before the writers' conference.

I said, "Yes. Yes, I can."

The rest, as they say, is... well... is written above in reverse chronological order.

If you're clever, and I know you are, I'll bet you picked up on two very important themes throughout my little tale.

The first, and probably the most important, is that everyone who read my work liked how I wrote and the way I crafted stories. I know it sounds like a no-brainer, but **you must be good at the craft of writing to be successful as a writer**. True, life doesn't *always* work that way. We've all read horribly written stories by massively successful writers. But I don't want to be a massively successful writer of crappy stories. And I hope you don't either. Bookstores have enough horribly written books.

Still, before I threw up that 9th novel of mine on my website, I had spent about fifteen years studying how to write stories and also... well... writing stories. Eight other novels before that one, if my math is accurate. And you know one fact about those eight other novels I wrote? No one will *EVER* read them. Why? Because they all suck! I was still learning how to write. That's what those eight novels were for – practice!

I want you to take a moment to understand what I'm saying here. The biggest issue I have with today's world of wannabe writers is the vast majority are trying to sell their *FIRST BOOK*!!!

And if that's you, you're not going to like what I have to say.

Because, *EVERYBODY'S FIRST BOOK SUCKS!!!*

Mine did. Yours does. Even Stephen King's first book sucked!!! It's just a fact.

But for some reason so many wannabe writers today write their *first book* and then try and force it down the industry's throat. And if you're reading this because you just wrote your first book and you're looking for advice on how to sell it, you won't find it from me. My advice is to write your next book because your *first* isn't good enough to sell. And yes, I get that your mommy told you it was the best little thing she's ever read in the whole wide world. But, trust me, she's lying to you. *Because she's your mom!* It's her job to lie to you.

Going back to my little tale. Everyone who read my work loved how I wrote and how I crafted stories. Not because I am smart, or talented, or gifted. If you know me, you know I'm none of those things. They loved my writing because **before I showed them my writing I had spent about fifteen years learning the craft of writing**.

I put in the time and effort *first*, *then* I started showing the world my ninth novel.

Meaning, when the industry read me, they liked what I wrote.

It really is that simple. Take the time and spend the effort to hone your craft before you try and become a professional writer. It will do wonders for your writing career.

But that's not the only message from my tale. The second half, and something that stops more wannabe writers from becoming professional writers than I care to speculate over, is what I did when those opportunities opened for me.

I said *YES!*

"Can you write movie scripts?"

"Yes."

"Can you write for a massive video game?"

"Yes."

"Can you teach writing in front of 600 people?"

"Yes."

"Can you meet me for dinner to discuss the book you're writing?"

"Yes."

Once you have the skill – and I mean *REALLY* have the skill and not just believe what your mother tells you about your skill – you will gain the confidence to *KNOW* you know what you're doing. So, when someone asks, "Can you write (fill in the blank)?" You can confidently answer, "Yes. Yes, I can."

Lesons learned:
- ✓ You must be good at the craft of writing to be successful as a writer.
- ✓ Everybody's first book sucks. Put it away, take what you've learned, and write the next book.
- ✓ Before I showed anyone my writing I had spent about fifteen years learning the craft of writing.
- ✓ When you have the skill – REALLY have the skill – you'll have the confidence to know you know what you're doing.

*

Maxwell Alexander Drake is an award-winning Science Fiction/Fantasy author, Graphic Novelist, and Playwright. He was also the Lead Fiction Writer and game story consultant for Sony's massive online game EverQuest Next *as well as writing for the* Shadowrun *game. He is best known for his fantasy series,* The Genesis of Oblivion Saga. *Drake teaches creative writing at writers' conferences and fan conventions all around the world, and is the author of the* Drake's Brutal Writing Advice *series.*

For more, please visit www.MaxwellAlexanderDrake.com, or his writing training website www.DrakeU.com. You can also follow him on Twitter @MaxwellADrake, on Facebook /MaxwellAlexanderDrake, or Instagram /MaxwellAlexanderDrake.

How I (Almost) Didn't Get Published

Martin Shoemaker

When I was 14 years old, I learned that *anyone* could send a story to *Isaac Asimov's Science Fiction Magazine* (which has since dropped "Isaac" from its name). They had just published a story from a 13-year-old author, so I should be fine, right? And I had placed in a couple of local youth writing contests. So I was excited to try.

Back in those dinosaur days, that meant typing my manuscript on my manual typewriter, laboriously marking up corrections for typos, typing a cover letter, putting both into an envelope along with a SASE (Self-Addressed Stamped Envelope), taking the package down to the post office, getting it weighed, paying for postage, mailing it… and waiting. And waiting…

And eventually I got my manuscript back, along with a form postcard with some box checked (I forget what it said) and a typed addition from editor George Scithers: "Puns generally don't work for us." (It was a really *stupid* pun.)

And then… Well, that was a *lot* of work to do for just a form response. Oh, sure, there was that additional typed line (making it what today I recognize as a personal rejection, but I didn't know what that meant – it was long before the internet, and I didn't know anybody who knew anything about the writing business). And although I'm *generally* very patient, I'm impatient when waiting for the mail. Plus I *hate* mailing things. Plus I was only 14, so I couldn't get to the post office myself. Plus, plus, plus...

Plus the rejection hurt. But I've never told anyone that before. *Anyone.* You're the first, because I think you'll understand.

So I gave up. I still kept writing, but I gave up on submitting. Besides, I'd discovered two things: computer programming, and role-playing games. I enjoyed both, and they satisfied some of the same creative urges as writing. So they distracted me. (And *then* I discovered girls! Talk about distractions...) Plus it looked possible that computer programming could become a career. I was good at it, and it paid good money.

So I gave up on submitting (*not* on writing)... until age 21, when I wrote a longer, D&D-inspired story that I really thought had potential. At that time, *Amazing Stories* was owned by TSR, the makers of D&D (that's *Dungeons and Dragons* for those of you who aren't role-players). The story seemed like a natural fit there. So again with the typing and the correcting and the cover lettering and the enveloping and the driving and the weighing and the paying and the mailing. And the waiting.

And again with the rejection. (Again from George Scithers, who by then had moved over to *Amazing*.) And again it hurt. So again I gave up.

Besides, by then I was already working as a computer programmer. Thirty-six years later I still am. I'm *good* at it, and it's a good career. Along the way I also wrote a book *and* a comic strip on software design. I wrote and taught classes on software design. Software development is a really good home for me.

Yet still I kept writing fiction. I bought lots of books on writing, and I kept trying. And submitting. I've lost track of the details, but there were a few more submissions and a few more rejections in there. Every time it hurt, and every time I gave up.

When I was 47, I wrote *Scramble*, which I thought was the first chapter of a novel. (Someday...) My brother-in-law Mark (a voracious reader even among a family of readers) read it and said, "That's not a chapter, that's a short story. Send it out." So I sent it out to *Asimov's*. And after a few months... they rejected it.

And then something changed. I wish I knew what it was. I suspect it's simply that I matured (i.e., I grew up) to the point where rejection didn't hurt... as much. I sent *Scramble* to another market. I wrote and submitted lots more stories. I researched markets. I researched writing books and courses and critique groups. I kept at it. I persisted.

For six whole months!

And then... I gave up. Because if six months wasn't enough, it wasn't going to happen, right? (Please don't judge me...) So I told myself that on January 1, I would give up on writing, and instead try to make money writing Windows Phone games. (Please don't judge me...)

But until then...

One of my writing mentors, Dean Wesley Smith, had tried to hammer into me Heinlein's business rules for writing:

You must write.

You must finish what you start.

You must refrain from rewriting except to editorial order.

You must put it on the market.

You must keep it on the market until sold.

I was already following rule 1. And I was *mostly* following rule 2. (No writer finishes *everything*. Sometimes writing is just practice.)

But rule 3? Are you crazy? Everyone knows that writing is rewriting! You've got to be wrong, Dean! (Spoiler alert: no, he's not. At least not for some writers.)

But Dean convinced me to try. What did I have to lose? I was getting ready to give up anyway, right? So why waste time rewriting if I was going to give up?

So I followed rule 3 *and* rule 4. I had written *The Mother Anthony*, a nice little piece inspired by Jack McDevitt's *Echo*. Rather than endlessly rewrite it, I just sent it out to *Asimov's*.

And then there's rule 5: Keep it on the market. Dean's advice was when a story comes back rejected, send it out again immediately. But I get busy, so I compromised: every Saturday night, every story in my inventory had to be out to a market. If it wasn't, send it out! (Electronically... No SASE, no weighing, no postage... You kids these days have it sooooo easy... Get off my lawn, you rotten kids!) I had promised Dean, so I stuck to the rule; but

January 1 was coming, so I only had to hold out a little longer before I stopped wasting my time.

I was actually looking forward to giving up. To the relief of not trying, not hoping any more. *The Mother Anthony* came back from *Asimov's*, rejected. On a Saturday. December 31. One more day. I had no choice: by my own rules, I had to send it out one more time, to one more market. So I searched for a market.

And I found Writers of the Future. I didn't know what it was, just some sort of contest; but I knew that Dean spoke very highly of it. So did Jerry Pournelle, one of my all-time favorite writers. Both were judges for the contest. So I looked it up. It had a quarterly deadline; and the next deadline was... midnight. December 31. That night.

I *love* synchronicity. I don't ever expect it to work out, but I know it will make a great story if it does. So my last submission ever, ever, *ever,* on the very last day of the year, on the very last day of a quarterly contest? How could I resist? I submitted *The Mother Anthony* shortly before midnight.

And then (you should know where this is going by now) I gave up. I dug into learning Windows Phone programming. It was fun. I was good at it. It was fun. (Did I mention it was fun?) In rapid order, I wrote three games; and by late March, I had earned *fifty dollars* from my games!

Then I got a call from Joni Labaqui, contest coordinator for Writers of the Future, telling me that "The Mother Anthony" was a Finalist for the quarter.

And I didn't even remember submitting it!

I also didn't really understand the Contest, so I didn't understand that there were only eight Finalist stories per quarter out of thousands of submissions. I was honored, but... I went back to my Windows Phone games.

And then Joni called again a month later. *The Mother Anthony* hadn't won; but Jerry Pournelle had loved it. He thought it should've won.

Jerry Pournelle. I have books of his all over my shelves. And he loved my story.

And that's when I gave up giving up.

I decided that maybe what was holding me back was simply my fear of rejection; and maybe if I didn't let rejection stop me, I could get somewhere. I sent some of my old stories out to some new markets.

Within a month, I sold *The Night We Flushed the Old Town* to *Digital Science Fiction*, a small pro-paying magazine. Two months later, I sold them *Father-Daughter Outing* as well.

About a year later, I sold *Not Close Enough* to *Analog Science Fiction & Fact*, the longest-running science fiction magazine still in print.

Scramble took second place in the Jim Baen Memorial Writing Contest, sponsored by Baen Books. That didn't get my story published; but the first-place winner, Richard Johnson, asked me to attend the ceremony (he couldn't fly there from Australia) and read his speech. There I had lunch with *Buzz Aldrin!* I also heard him talk about his Mars Cycler program; and I turned that idea into *Murder on the Aldrin Express* three months later. *Analog* bought that not long after.

The next year I sold *Il Gran Cavallo* and *Pallbearers* to *Galaxy's Edge*.

And I was still submitting to Writers of the Future! The contest is open only to amateurs. Professionals, as defined by more than three sales to SFWA-qualified pro markets, are ineligible they "pro out", as we say in the Writers of the Future Forum). But neither *Digital Science Fiction* nor *Galaxy's Edge* were SFWA-qualified at the time, so those sales didn't count as far as the contest was concerned. I was still an "amateur", even though I had been paid.

Then Gardner Dozois selected *Murder on the Aldrin Express* for his annual *Year's Best Science Fiction* collection. I emailed Joni and said, "I don't think I'll count as an amateur after this comes out. I think this will have to be my last quarter." And Joni answered, "Then you'd better win it."

And I did! *Unrefined* took third place in the first quarter for Volume 31, winning me prize money, a workshop with pro authors who are now my mentors (and my friends!), an *amazing* illustration by Jessica T.C. Lee, and another pro sale.

All because after 34 years, I gave up giving up.

I've now got 33 short fiction sales (and one poetry sale, coming soon). My short story *Today I Am Paul* was nominated for a Nebula Award, awarded the Washington Science Fiction Small Press Award, has been reprinted in *four* different year's best collections, and translated into eight languages. I've turned that story into a novel, *Today I Am Carey*, from Baen Books, and my next novel, *The Last Dance*, will be out from 47North in November, 2019. And there's more to come!

All because I gave up giving up.

Heinlein's Rules seem to work for me. Sometimes they don't.

Pantsing (i.e., writing by the seat of my pants) seems to work for me. But sometimes I outline.

Sometimes I write short. Sometimes I write long. Sometimes I write funny. Sometimes I write sad. Sometimes I write nuts-n-bolts hard science fiction, sometimes I write space opera, and sometimes I write fantasy. Sometimes it works, and sometimes it doesn't. I never know what will work.

But what I know will *not* work is: giving up.

So I want to save you the thirty years of time I spent wishing, but afraid to try. I'm not going to lie, not here in this book: rejection hurts! But wishing and regretting hurts, too. And that's a longer hurt – one that never goes away. Every time you read a book, you'll remember what you might have done, had you dared. Every time you look at that stack of old manuscripts (or that folder full of manuscript files, for you rotten kids on my lawn), you'll feel the ache.

As John Greenleaf Whittier wrote: *"For of all sad words of tongue or pen, The saddest are these: 'It might have been!'"*

I'm not making promises! You can try and try your whole life and never once find your audience. It's sad, but it happens. There are no promises in this business, no guarantees.

No guarantees save one. As Robert A. Heinlein wrote: "Certainly the game is rigged. Don't let that stop you; if you don't bet you can't win." The one way to be *sure* you won't succeed is to give up.

There's no shame in giving up. Only you can decide what's right for you, what you really want.

But it's time for more honest sharing that I've never shared with anyone else. Not my friends, not my family, not my fellow writers, not my wife. I've even lied about it so people don't feel sorry for me. But I share it with you because I want you to see that you're not much different from published writers. It's this: though I generally live by a "no regrets" philosophy, figuring that my life overall is pretty good... sometimes I regret what I might have written in all those years I wasted on giving up.

So if you really want to write... Please don't be like me. Don't give up!

Lesons learned:
- ✓ Rejection hurts. So does regret, and it lasts longer.
- ✓ Every writer you've ever read knows that rejection hurts. They've had plenty. And they didn't let it stop them. You shouldn't, either.
- ✓ A *personal* rejection means that a very busy editor with hundreds of stories to reject that month saw something special in your work. They took time to encourage you. Send them more stories.
- ✓ When you get a rejection, send that story out again to the next market immediately. And write your next story.
- ✓ Don't be like me. Don't give up.

*

Martin L. Shoemaker is a programmer who writes on the side... or maybe it's the other way around. Programming pays the bills, but a second place story in the Jim Baen Memorial Writing Contest earned him lunch with Buzz Aldrin. Programming never did that! His work has appeared in Analog *several times, as well as in* Galaxy's Edge, Digital Science Fiction, Forever Magazine, *and* Writers of the Future. *His* Clarkesworld *story,* Today I Am Paul, *appeared in four different year's best anthologies and eight international editions. His follow-on novel,* Today I Am Carey, *was published by Baen Books in 2019.*

One Brick Does Not
A House Make

(Just As Writing Alone Does Not A Career Make)

Raymond Bolton

I am directing this essay at authors who are looking for more than getting one book into print, and who are also looking to start a career as a traditionally published author. So, rather than simply regaling you with an uplifting and encouraging tale about how I found a publisher, I am assembling this like a "How To" manual because, in and of itself, my story won't help get you published, but the elements that got me there might. Some of them are obvious. A few are less so. But I strongly suspect that some that were crucial to my success, would never occur to you.

I'm also certain you will tell yourself, "I could never do that." And perhaps you're right... but maybe you should try, because the two obvious exceptions are remarkable tools for separating yourself from the crowd in a market that is being deluged with millions of titles.

I'd always wanted to write a book, always wanted to see my name in print. At various points in my life I had visions of completing a grand story, then sending it off to some agent or publisher who would fall in love with it, after which I'd become a bestselling author. It happened like that to a friend of mine:

romance author, Brenda Joyce. Her debut novel, *Innocent Fire*, was a runaway bestseller that sold out in a matter of weeks. Almost immediately afterwards, she signed on with a larger publishing house. Forty five novels later, she's become one of her genre's celebrities.

My path to publishing took years longer and was exceedingly convoluted. Several lessons I learned along the way helped me find my eventual publisher. Pardon me if the first lesson sounds like I'm preaching, but it is the cornerstone upon which a writing career is built, the most important and universally applicable.

Master Your Craft and Learn What Publishers Require

Who among us would sit down at a piano and with no practice at all, bang away on the keys, then announce, "I am a concert pianist"? Everyone knows you can't even begin to think about becoming a concert pianist without years of practice, years perfecting your technique, years mastering what the greats have composed.

Writing is no different.

I began writing my debut novel in the midst of a disintegrating marriage. We had nothing to say to each other when we got home at night, so I spent the time writing. With no previous instruction on how to compose a novel and only the vaguest idea as to structure, the first draft became a 174,000 word behemoth. It was years in the making because I needed to learn how to spin epic fantasy.

When it was done, the ending sucked. My wife told me so. I was tired of writing and just wrapped it up. I'd slaved over a gourmet dinner, then threw handfuls onto plates saying, "There. It's done. Now eat it." Three attempts later, my wife assured me the ending worked, but insisted it was too verbose. Nonetheless, I sent it out.

Among the "not for us" rejection slips, I did receive some praise. *"Your writing is good. It moves forward."* Less strong was, *"It almost knocked me out."* Bunts. No homer. Further, those who spared the time to pen a note all pointed to the manuscript's word count. My baby needed slimming.

I reduced it to 147K, agonizing over the disappearance of so much hard work. When one agent said she'd give it a look if I pared it to 125 thousand, I exceeded her request to no avail. The problem was the writing. It wasn't bad, but it wasn't great. Good doesn't cut it if you want a publisher or agent to sit back and take notice.

So I studied. I studied Ernest Hemmingway's compact prose, Dean Koontz's elegant turn of a phrase and Jacqueline Carey's imagery knowing someday, once my skills improved, the gem within would emerge. Writing, however, takes time to mature. I shelved the project, wrote two more novels, changing genre in the process.

All the while, the epic refused to remain sleeping, tugging at my consciousness, demanding my attention. It needed to be told. I thought, "this is not how an inadequate story behaves," so after several years' absence, I returned to it, tweaking and caressing, allusion replacing declaration, one word replacing several. The sentences became clearer, leaner, but not sparse. They were stronger for it. If you're seeking a traditional publisher, your agent, your publisher, and ultimately your readers will demand nothing less than a professional showing.

Eventually my manuscript's word count matched most publishers' requirements. They require a first novel to be between 80,000 and 90,000 words in length. Historical novels or epic fantasies should run between 100K-120K. My finished manuscript weighed in at a trim 109,228 words.

Develop A Community

Successful writers do not work in a vacuum. Community is everything.

When I started out, I was the only author I knew, would-be or otherwise. I spent years floundering, trying to learn anything about the publishing industry. Fortunately for me, before I was published I worked as a high-end hairdresser and a large number of successful people, some of them authors, found their way into my chair. These days, I suggest new writers join online author groups through social media, something that wasn't around when I started writing.

One of my author clients was Dennis Tedlock, McNulty Professor of English and Research Professor of Anthropology at the State University of New York at Buffalo and first credible translator of *The Popol Vuh*, the Mayan equivalent of the Rosetta Stone. He and his wife, Barbara, another author of note, introduced me to PEN New Mexico, where I briefly served as Treasurer and met several other authors who suggested I attend writers' conferences.

At their urgings, in 2010 I flew from Santa Fe, New Mexico to Seattle, Washington to attend the Pacific Northwest Writers Association's annual summer conference. It was attended by over 650 writers, as well as several dozen agents and editors, and it is where I met published romance author and sci-fi/fantasy fan, Kate Austin. We launched into a series of communications, one of which resulted in her editing my novel, *Thought Gazer*, for entry into PNWA's annual literary competition. One of her major suggestions was to completely eliminate the first chapter, in order to start it off at the story's true beginning – something I never would have recognized on my own.

This leads me to the next lesson:

You are an inadequate judge of your work. Find *qualified* critics, and learn to accept their instruction.

I gave the original manuscript of my epic fantasy, *Thought Gazer*'s predecessor, to several friends, hoping they would provide valuable insights. Friends, however, tend to respond with "It's a nice book" and nothing more for fear of offending you, if they even bother to read what you give them. However, when one of my clients turned out to be the iconic former *Redbook Magazine* editor, Audreen Buffalo, things took a different turn.

Over the course of our association, I had the opportunity to present small snippets of my work to her, largely poetry. She expressed her enjoyment, so I found the nerve to tell her about my completed manuscript. When she offered to read and critique it – for a fee, of course – I found a way to come up with the money.

Audreen taught me many of the basics, like the importance of active, rather than passive sentences – "He kicked the ball" is more dynamic than "The ball was kicked by him" – among many other invaluable lessons that followed, all of which I adhered to.

Submit your manuscript to literary competitions.

While most competitions only accept short stories, a few are intended for book length works. The Pacific Northwest Writers

Association's annual literary competition is one such. Hundreds of authors participate, so the odds of your winning are initially small. But because, win or lose, you receive critiques from successful authors in your genre, if you will accept what they tell you, your writing will improve.

So it was that in 2013, after several earlier failed attempts, I submitted my debut novel under the working title, *Renunciation*, competing with more than 950 other manuscripts, where it became one of eight finalists. That convinced me that my story had developed to the point I ought to publish it. And though I still could not convince any agent to accept me as their client, self-publishing was just taking off, so I decided to risk going that route.

Don't settle for less than a first rate, professionally designed cover.

As I prepared to launch *Awakening*, as I finally named it, I realized that one way to encourage potential readers to buy it was to make it as physically attractive as possible, knowing that readers would link the quality of the book's content to its presentation. To find an appropriate artist, I turned to a Facebook authors' group whose founding member was a New York Times bestseller. I was always taken by the consistently superior quality of her books' covers, so I asked if she would put me in touch with the artist. When she obliged, and her artist agreed to work with me, I braced myself for what I expected would be a phenomenally high fee.

To my surprise, I found she was very affordable. I was also delighted by how quickly we arrived at a satisfactory design. After three of her submissions, followed by my suggestions for changes that would reflect the story better, she presented a cover that members of that author group likened to a movie poster.

Find readers by contributing to the success of other authors.

Because of the effort I had put into *Awakening*, it began earning mostly five star reviews, averaging 4.7 stars across the Internet, as it still does today. Even so, it soon became lost among the millions of titles that were finding their way into the marketplace, and I began searching for tools to make it more prominent. Blog tours that had previously been successful were now having little impact on sales. Television and radio interviews helped somewhat, but sales remained anything but stellar.

In the course of scouring the Internet for suggestions as to how I might use my new website – designed, by the way, by my cover artist – to promote my work, I came across one piece of wisdom I still employ today: Don't ask readers to buy your book. Instead, promote other authors and their readers will respond appropriately. Admittedly, I thought the concept was odd, but with nothing to lose I launched an author interview series.

Since I didn't know any published authors of note, I began by featuring award-winning indie authors from the group I belonged to. They, like me, were craving whatever publicity they could find. I hoped this would also work to my advantage because, as their fans visited my website, they would see my books prominently featured on the sidebar and "Books" page.

By late 2014, I knew I had started drawing serious attention, because several months into the series I received an email from an author's publicist asking if I would showcase her client. This was not just any author, mind you. This was Hank Phillippi Ryan, NBC Boston's on-air investigative reporter with 32 Emmys and 12 Edward R. Murrows to her credit, along with dozens of other honors for her ground-breaking journalism. Moreover, Ryan had won multiple prestigious awards for her crime fiction novels: the Agatha, Anthony, Macavity, and the coveted Mary Higgins Clark Award. Naturally, I accepted. That interview gave me enough credibility that I was soon featuring other notables. including Robert Dugoni, Jake Needham, and Anne Hillerman.

Consider having your book translated into another language.

While searching for ways to expand my sales, I stumbled across an article informing me that many authors were having their books translated into other languages, primarily German and Spanish, because far fewer books were available in those markets and it was easier to attract readers' attention. Since no one I knew spoke German, and since I was living in Santa Fe, I decided to look into Spanish as a possibility.

I soon learned that (1) Spanish is the most widely spoken language on earth, (2) there is a long history of Hispanic books involving fantasy, my preferred genre, running from Miguel de Cervantes to Gabriel García Márquez, and (3) Spanish Language readers are craving books in their native tongue.

I was also told that, when searching for a translator, it is imperative that individual be a native speaker educated at the university level. I was delighted then, when once of my clients introduced me to a friend of hers, even more so when Joaquín Font, born in Barcelona with a Masters Degree from Harvard University, certified to translate in Federal Court, and CEO of Font Translations, expressed interest. Once we had arrived at a suitable arrangement, Joaquín, uncertain he could bring enough literary quality to the work, assigned the primary translation to Sylvia Vásquez, a published poet from Puerto Rico.

Despite their qualifications, they made some early missteps. When one of my characters exclaimed, "What in the world have you been doing?", they translated it as, "What have you been doing in the world?" Consequently, I enlisted Carole Chávez Hunt, a native English speaker and professor of Spanish at a college in Santa Fe.

As a result of the translation's quality and because there are so few books in Spanish available online, when Amazon published it, *El despertar* immediately became the number one new release in ciencia ficción.

Press the flesh. Put yourself in front of readers by purchasing a dealer's table at as many cons as you can afford.

Sitting alone in your office will get your books written, but it's a poor way to market yourself. There is no better way to put your work into the hands of readers than by meeting them face-to-face and telling them what you've written.

In 2014, almost as soon as *Awakening* was available, I began selling it at book fairs and events like Westercon and Rose City Comic Con. In response, there was a modest increase in online sales, since many conference attendees inquire about ebook availability, and my books were available in ePub and Kindle formats.

When I learned that WorldCon was coming to Spokane, Washington in 2015, I nearly leapt out of my chair. Friends had remarked that their books had flown off their tables at LonCon in

2014 and I envisioned similar results at Sasquan, WorldCon's Spokane incarnation.

Little did I suspect what that event held in store for me.

I ordered several cases of my two existing English language titles, *Awakening* and *Thought Gazer*. Because WorldCon is an international event drawing attendees from several nations, I also brought a handful of copies of *El despertar*.

Two weeks before the event, I was checking the arrangements I had made when I realized I hadn't booked a hotel room. In a panic, I went online, only to learn that all of the affordable rooms had been taken and only a few were left at the Davenport Hotel, Spokane's costliest. But since I also learned that this was where many of the conference's notables were hanging their hats, I decided to accept my situation with a degree of optimism.

The first thing I noticed when I entered the hotel lobby was a poster announcing that WordFire Press was throwing a book launch party that very night for Nebula and multiple Hugo Award winning author, Mike Resnick. Had I stayed somewhere else, I would never have known about it. With nothing in mind beyond the possibility of booking an interview, I decided to attend.

Fortunately for me, Mike was fashionably late. Since I had no idea what he looked like, I sought out the person in charge of the event. As soon as I made my purpose known, I was surrounded by WordFire's authors, all of whom were handing me their business cards and hoping I would feature them as well... no small bonus for me, as I was always looking for interviewees.

I'm pleased to say that Mr. Resnick couldn't have been more open to what I was proposing, even offering to put me in touch with his daughter, Laura Resnick, who is also an author. At one point, he looked across the room and said, "There's Nancy Kress. I'll introduce you to her."

Mike and Nancy became the first science fiction authors I interviewed. Their names paved the way for others like Alan Dean Foster, Seanan McGuire, Charles Gannon, Jody Lynn Nye, and Sherrilyn Kenyon. As I had hoped, many of their fans have since visited my website and are now on my mailing list. Moreover, a few of these authors have reciprocated by reading and endorsing my work.

It didn't stop there. At one point, Alexi Vandenberg, WordFire's publicist, dropped by my author table on the conference floor and examined what I was selling. Unexpectedly, he picked up a copy of *El despertar*, opened it to the beginning of a chapter, read the first paragraph, then looked up at me. "We will talk," he said without further explanation, but I had an idea what he was getting at. He purchased a copy, then later had his assistant drop by and pick up the English version.

I could not have anticipated that Spanish was Alexi's native tongue, but other readers also scooped it up before even starting to look at *Awakening.* At one point, when Alexi learned I would have a table at Rose City Comic Con a few weeks later, he asked me to look him up, saying that WordFire Press would be there as well.

It turned out that WordFire was throwing a party for their authors at Starbuck's in Portland's Pearl District and Alexi invited me to attend. There, he introduced me to Kevin J. Anderson, WordFire's owner, and Peter Wachs, WordFire's then acquisitions editor, praising *Awakening*'s virtues to both.

The publishing industry, however, moves at a glacial pace and months went by without any word from them one way or another. At one point, I decided to be the squeaky wheel and gave Peter a poke. He informed me he had left WordFire, but promised to encourage their new acquisitions editor, Dave Butler, to take a look at my book.

Finally, in September, 2016, I received an email from Kevin in which he told me that Dave was insisting that WordFire acquire *Awakening*, and "without any developmental edits", adding, "Do you know how rare that is?" Further, when WordFire published it, they changed exactly three words, even deciding to retain the self-published version's cover, making only minor changes to it. Do you know how rare *that* is?

All the effort I'd put into making the book as perfect as possible, inside and out, paid off in a manner that reflected it to the extent that, when they also acquired the prequel trilogy that began with *Thought Gazer*, they did so with no developmental edits either and retained those covers as well.

Today, *El despertar* is the only title of mine that remains self-published, but I now entertain hopes it will not remain so much longer. In September, 2019, Latino Literacy Now awarded it medals for Best Fantasy/Science Fiction Novel In Spanish and Best Translation From English Into Spanish at the International Latino Book Awards in Los Angeles, California. This is the same organization that awarded medals to Isabel Allende, Paolo Coelho, Gabriel García Márquez and Supreme Court Justice Sonia Sotomayor. Because the International Latino Book Awards was attended by several Spanish Language publishers, I have high expectations one of them will acquire it as well.

Lesons learned:

All of this is because I:

- ✓ Mastered my craft and learned what publishers require,
- ✓ Developed a community,
- ✓ Found qualified critics and learned to accept their instruction,
- ✓ Submitted my work to literary competitions,
- ✓ Found readers by contributing to the success of other authors,
- ✓ Had my book translated into another language, and
- ✓ Purchased a dealer's table at as many conferences as I could afford.

*

Raymond Bolton lives near Portland, Oregon with his wife, Toni, and their cats, Max and Arthur. He is endlessly curious about the world around him and what he can do while he's still on it. Over the years he's driven trucks, been an FM disk jockey, produced concerts, served as a mainsail trimmer on racing yachts, piloted gliders, written software, worked as a hair stylist and owned and operated his own business. More recently, he has published five novels, initially as self-published works, four of which have since been acquired by WordFire Press, publisher of the Dune *series of novels.*

Skeletons in my Closet
M.K. Drake

I've got it! This is brilliant! Where is my laptop! Need to get writing straight away!

We've all been there. The moment when an idea for a story strikes true. That feeling you have when that little spark of a story arc is born. It's almost like raising a baby. It begins all cheery and happy, but can get really messy faster than an orange bloke posting a tweet.

I remember my moment. I wanted to get writing straight away, I was expecting everything to just flow. *Write it and they will come*, the words that is. But they didn't. The idea I had was too big, too ambitious, I needed time. And I pretty well took it.

From inception to the release of my first book, was ten years in the making. Ten years of planning, ten years of having an overall arc that would span nine to ten books, plus spin offs. It gave me many headaches. But during those years, I was still learning. Yes, I was confident in creating a *story*, but I had no idea how to plan a *novel*, even though the ideas were all in my head and scattered notes. Technology changes quickly, and in the space of those ten years I had amalgamated written notes, emails, text messages and voice memos. All of these were small jigsaw puzzle pieces for the whole picture. A picture I was starting to really dislike.

And it was this dislike that pushed me towards my first major mistake: I was so eager to just get started, I thought I was good enough to get going and begin the story.

I had the arc, I felt the story would just write itself. And in some ways it did. Atticus was born!

And then it wasn't.

*

The problem with taking so long to get started is that some of the ideas you had way back when, may be created in all their glory in other books – or a movie – before you get to them. One example I experienced was The Kraken.

In my first book, I had planned to feature The Kraken as one of the big foes. A formidable creature for sure, and I was excited to get this monstrous adversary against my heroes. Alas, by the time I started writing the book, it was at the time of the release of the second *Pirates of the Caribbean* movie, which featured the fearsome mythological creature in full CGI glory. I was distraught. I thought I would be accused of being a copycat, even though I had already had this idea years before the movie came about.

I therefore changed direction, midway through the book. I had to think of a new foe, equally as formidable and tweak some of the research I had already carried out. What could strike as much fear into the souls of man as The Kraken? I finally decided on the biblical Leviathan, but with a twist. I played heavily on Norse mythology in the first book, so hinted at a link that Leviathan and Jörmungandr were one and the same. I felt it worked well. And I was content again.

I created characters that *I* knew so well. I gave them personalities that *I* knew so well. I gave them an appearance that *I* could see so well. Remember the italicised 'I's' here. They will be important for later.

Off I went, into the ether, into the crazy world of writing a story. I checked sites such as the *Writers Workshop* for tips. Looked at other books in my genre, and then it was finally time. I thought I was ready to embark on this adventure. My book was being born! My baby! I wrote and wrote, I used chapter titles as my only guide to get me to the end. I got to the point where everything was just working well, words were flowing, chapters were episodic as planned. And then I stalled. I started to doubt what I had. I hit a block. The writer's version of a marathon runner's wall.

I was full of self-doubt. I stopped writing for a year. Somehow, I managed to complete the first draft. I thought it was good, and I sent it for an independent paid review with the *Writer's Workshop*, where I waited eagerly for glowing praise to come back.

In the meantime, I also sent this ugly duckling to a few trusted friends to read. They mostly came back with glowing praise, saying that they loved the story... all but one. He was candid, and said to my face he didn't like it at all. I appreciated his honesty, but it was also the first time I had received negative feedback. How could my trusted friend slaughter my work in such a way?

I took solace in the feedback from those that had contained nothing but positivity, giving me more confidence. I needed it to boost my own ego. I had written perfection! I was king!

And then the independent review came back.

They praised many things, but they also tore the book apart. They told me that the structure of the story was all over the place. The characters were one-dimensional. And it was too much like Harry Potter!

I was livid. How dare this person tell me such things after a decade of work. But then I remembered what my friend with a dissenting voice against the horde of praise had said.

And they were similar observations.

So, I decided to read my *masterpiece* again, with the words of dissent and criticism ringing through my mind. And you know what? They were right.

Blinded by my own imagining of the world that *I* knew, the characters *I* knew, the story *I* knew, I had forgotten to tell the story to someone that *didn't* know those things.

All of those 'I's' were catching up with me. How do I fix this? How do I make it right?

*

Things were made worse when a former work colleague suddenly made it big with his own story series. He was finding great success, and I must admit to feeling a little bit jealous. I was immensely proud of my friend, incredibly happy for him, but I wanted some of that success, too.

And that is when it really dawned on me. I had forgotten why I wanted to write in the first place. I was trying to force success, focussing far too much on that than the actual story.

I reminded myself of why I'm doing this. It was a cold hard realisation. *You must love to write.* You have to enjoy it. I had forgotten that. And that was when I realised that these stories I write aren't really for me, they are for everyone out there. They are for those that need to be inspired. They are for those that need to escape a normal world. They are there to create a sense of wonder. A sense of adventure.

It was the kick I needed to go back and look again. I re-structured the book, created a proper arc with a beginning, a middle and an end, and rewrote the story.

I focused more on writing the characters as I knew them, and not expecting the reader to already do so. I gave them more time to express themselves and expanded on their backgrounds and personalities. I looked at how to control perspective much better. My style of using the present tense was not to everyone's liking, but it was my style and I decided to stick with it and work to make it less intrusive. My wonderful editor helped me immensely with this.

I learnt so much. And when I felt it was ready, I asked my newly published friend for advice. He freely gave it, and it was how I found Camden Park Press for the first time.

I booked my slot for the edit, and waited with baited breath.

I was on tenterhooks, and then the email arrived. My edited manuscript had returned. And this time, it was not torn to shreds. There was praise and incredibly useful edits. I had grown immensely, not only as a writer, but the experience helped me grow as a person, too. I knew why I wanted to write.

I finally launched *Atticus & The Orb of Time* in January 2015.

But I couldn't stop there, I still had at least another nine books for the series that I had to write!

However, I wanted to do it better. I needed to learn from my previous mistakes. I consulted with my editor, and she advised several things.

*

One of the most important bits I learned was ensuring you have the skeleton right. Not just of your story arc, but of your characters, too – especially when you're writing a series.

Keep a spreadsheet of them all, this has been so invaluable! I have such a vast array of characters in my stories that, without this, I would be completely lost! You need to keep their profiles there, almost like the biographies you read on gaming character cards.

I started with this. And then I wrote my first skeleton. The overall story arc for *Atticus & The Scrolls Of The Pharaoh*!

I had my beginning, my middle and my end planned out. I had the synopsis there in all its glory. So I thought I was ready to go again. Let's get this second instalment out there! I revved up my engines, turned on Word... and I stopped. I asked myself, "Is this enough?"

It wasn't.

This was possibly one of the most important steps I took to get to where I am now: I went back to the main arc, and dissected it.

And then I created a much more detailed skeleton. I then went even deeper.

I created chapter titles as I did before for the first book, but this time I ensured they aligned with the newly detailed structure.

The next step was to create a detailed synopsis for each chapter. I did this all the way through; it was a brilliant mechanism!

I knew where the story was going, but I was able to tweak on the fly. I could adapt the story as new ideas flew into my mind.

Oh! One major piece of advice, *always* have some way to send yourself reminders. I've lost count of how many times a genius idea has been victim to the nothingness of forgotten memories... all because I didn't have something with me to write it down with, or send an email with, or just do anything with.

I now sleep with my phone within reach!

Trust me, when that middle of the night idea wakes you up, the idea that may well illuminate itself in a dream, you will not remember it in the morning. Send that email, make that note, leave yourself a voicemail. You will thank me later for it.

Anyhow, I now had my first proper skeleton for the story. I had my character profiles. I had conviction and purpose.

I managed to get the first draft of my second book completed six months after I had completed the skeletal overview! I was amazed at how much having that structure in place helped. And that first draft was so good that it was crazily similar to the version that launched. Having that skeleton helped me shape the story to a level I knew I wanted from the very beginning. It helped me with pacing things so much better than before.

After the nightmare journey of my first book, this was an absolute revelation. I think I actually danced a jig – and I think that might be what triggered my sciatic nerve pain. It was bloody well worth it though.

I was so much more confident with this book. I knew it had much more purpose and quality than my first. I really felt I had grown as a writer. I had taken on the lessons of the past, and used them to create something better.

The feedback was coming through thick and fast. I was eager to get to work on book three, but alas, work and life delayed me immensely.

I was starting to get disheartened. Then I received a message from one reader, reminding me again of why I write.

She said that while the genre of my series was not usually her go-to one, she wanted to thank me. She said that although my stories were not really for her, she was so happy – because my books had inspired her two teenage daughters to read. They had read the Atticus series and then gone on to a journey of literary discovery.

This moment changed me completely. It reminded me why I started this crazy journey. It gave me the boost I needed. I damn well got back on that saddle and rode off into the sunset of twilight words, and only returned when I knew I had to change things!

What, again!

Yes, again. But this was very much down to the learnings of using the skeleton method to structure the story.

I originally intended for the Atticus series to be split into three trilogies. But as I structured the third book, it became hugely apparent that it was going to be far too long to keep within a manageable space of not just time, but also costs.

Yes, I'm writing for the love of writing, but being an indie published author, one needs to ensure that what you have is marketable and easy to read, without pricing yourself out of the market.

If the book is too long, nobody will give a second glance to your paperback, as the cost of printing would make it just too expensive.

I also felt that the story itself would benefit from being split into two books rather than one.

If I didn't use the skeleton method, I would have fallen down a slippery, and most likely, endless slope. The book would never have seen daylight for at least another two to three years.

This also allowed me to be even more creative. Splitting the book into two volumes gave me a little more room and space to let characters breathe. I could help more of them grow, and become as good a friend of the reader as they are now of mine.

I had taken those lessons and used them to start submissions again. I was confident enough in my work that I sent my first two books to potential publishing houses.

And I had a bite!

A publishing house in Las Vegas of all places wanted me on their books. The contract looked relatively sound, but I wasn't quite happy with some of the terms. I took some time to get legal advice, and they made some adjustments for me. I also reached out to my editor and a few other writers.

They all said the same: *if you're not happy with the offer, you don't have to accept it*. So, I decided not to. You do not have to jump at the first offer. If you're lucky enough to get one, make sure it is right for you.

Since then I've not pursued the mainstream publishing market. I may do so again in the future. But right now, I'm just enjoying the fun of writing. It is a wonderful thing to be able to express yourself with words. To build magical worlds, to create stories of so much adventure that kids who have read the books come up to you and tell you they can't wait for the next instalment. To read that you have inspired someone's teenage daughters to pick up a book, turn a page, and not stop turning... those are truly enchanted things.

And to think, I learnt much of this during my journey of how to use a skeleton properly. All of those interconnecting bones. Who'da *thunk* it?

*

And you know what else I did? I bloody well used the Kraken in my third book. And he was spectacular!

This was a really good lesson for me, too. Do not pander to what you think others may think. Believe in your idea, believe in your story.

These pitfalls that I've been through, creating these stories, have all taught me to believe in myself, to have courage.

Write your story, it's what you want to tell. Do not fear what others are doing. Do not fear telling everyone about your world. Do not fear the naysayers. When asked why, reply, "Because I dared to!" Your own words will help give you that bravery.

Remember the moment you had that spark. That moment when you knew you had something special. Nurture it. Use it. Let it grow.

If I still feared the fact that a mythical beast used in many other stories already, was a no-go area just because it had appeared in a movie... well, I'd probably be the one who deserves to be locked away in Davy Jones's chest.

That fear is difficult to overcome, it perpetuates self-doubt. You sometimes wonder, "Am I really worthy? Am I really a writer?"

I say, you wouldn't be a writer if you didn't ask yourself those very questions. I could probably guarantee you that every single author, journalist, poet, singer, artist... they've all asked if they are worthy. What you don't want to do is give up. Take your dream and you damn well run with it. Shout it from the rooftops and tell your damn story. Sing your damn song and paint your dreams so the world sees them.

Everyone has the right to create. Everyone.

It's what makes us worthy, the beauty of being able to create the amazing. To inject an emotion so strong that you make someone else feel, shed a tear, smile. To make someone else pick up a pen, and write their story.

We share in our creativity the ability to show humanity what it is to be human. We have the ability to highlight wrongs and shine the spotlight on atrocities, in the hope that they do not happen again.

But we also have the ability to show what love is. What friendship is. What *human* truly is.

You have that power. You have that ability. You just need to believe it.

Just don't forget about those skeletal bones!

Lesons learned:
- ✓ Highlight the need to add structure to the story.
- ✓ Starting with a good structure really helps you form your arc.
- ✓ Learn the importance of the First, Second and Third act.
- ✓ Take notes when you get a Eureka moment.
- ✓ When you use known mythology, do not be too upset when elements of it appear in other media.
- ✓ Remember why you wanted to tell stories in the first place.

*

M.K. Drake is the author of the Atticus and the Majjai Six *series. He has currently published three of the ten book series and is busily underway writing the fourth. A father of two, he often acknowledges his children as his inspiration. Especially since his daughter believes he fights dragons for his day job. Unfortunately his day job is a tad more mundane being in the IT space.*

His love of fantasy and his mission to inspire others to pick up the pen are what drives him forward as well as his family. He hopes to one day be known for just that. The person who created worlds, to help others create their own. Follow his adventures on Facebook at https://www.facebook.com/atticusmajjaisix/

The Courage to Continue
Melissa McShane

I never intended to write fiction. I loved reading and talking about reading, and for many years I was a literary critic specializing in the analysis and celebration of fantasy literature, with an emphasis on young adult fantasy. I'd dabbled in writing fiction as I think most lovers of reading do, but never with any serious intent. Writing about the connections between readers and the books I loved was deeply satisfying, and I really did think I would do it forever.

When I was diagnosed with bipolar disorder type II in 2001, it was after months of depressive and manic episodes that left me not knowing who I really was. I assumed treatment would restore me to myself. Instead, I found myself shedding the things I loved as one by one they became too difficult to manage. Friends, volunteer work, homeschooling my children, even the literary organizations I was part of (and in one case was president of) fell away as I fought mental illness.

It took ten years for treatment to give me back my life. But it wasn't the life I'd had before. Even with the best treatment, with effective medication and therapy, I still dealt with that emotional cycle, and the medication had side effects that made me a different person.

At that point I felt adrift, full once more of energy and not knowing what to do with it. The organizations I'd left had moved on, and I didn't feel any of them had a place for me anymore. I wasn't famous – certainly not after ten years' absence – enough to make a career out of literary criticism, and it no longer appealed, anyway. Unfortunately, neither did anything else. I wrote some short stories, made a start on a couple of novels, but they felt uninspired and boring, and I didn't care enough to pursue it. When I finally completed a novel, it should have been cause for rejoicing, but instead I only felt tired. So I reached for other things.

I love making things. While my children were young, that took shape in crafts like painting, beadwork, and building models. After coming to myself, I went back to these crafts, but none of them filled the need I had to create something new, probably because I was usually following someone else's pattern. Every new thing captured my attention for a few weeks, maybe a month or two, and then I lost interest or decided I lacked the skills to be truly satisfied. I began to wonder if I was going to spend the rest of my life like a stereotypical '50s housewife, restlessly searching for meaning.

*

Sometime in 2013, frustrated and feeling hopeless, I had an idea for a book. Given that I had already failed at writing a novel, I didn't pay much attention to it. My first completed book had been dull and dully written, and it had felt like pulling teeth to get the ideas down. It was the wrong genre, the wrong concept, and had basically been a bad idea. But this new story – the main character, really – wouldn't go away. In desperation, and with the encouragement of my husband, I decided to try writing one more book. I think my feeling at the time was that I might as well do this as anything, and at least it wouldn't be an expensive failure. (I was not at my most positive.)

It turned out to be the best desperate move I ever made.

Unlike that first attempt, the words flowed, the idea was creative, and I enjoyed every minute of writing. To my surprise, it took only seven weeks to write the whole thing (the first one had been eight months of torture). After those seven weeks, I had a finished book – I, who had never thought of writing a book at all, had actually completed something! Even better, it was good – or at least nothing to be ashamed of. And best of all, I had felt incredible while writing it.

So I decided to see if I could do it again.

I am not one of those writers who complains about being pestered by the Idea Fairy, constantly filled with concepts for new projects. I have one idea at a time, and I always feel I will never write another book after I finish the last one. The second book was based on stories I'd told myself while falling asleep, stories that lacked something to pull them together. With some brainstorming help, I came up with a unified plot and wrote the book. It went even faster than the first and was even more fun because of my long-time love for the story.

And when it was finished, I realized I'd always wanted to tell a second story in that world – and the process started again.

I'd written five books in eight months before it occurred to me that maybe I should consider doing this as more than a hobby. I would have been satisfied with writing and sharing my books with no one other than friends and family, but I believed my books were good enough that other people might like them, too. I wanted to see if, having succeeded beyond imagining at actually completing a book, I could make a success out of the next step on the road.

I knew nothing about publishing beyond a vague awareness that e-books were a big thing (I read mainly print because my e-reader puts me to sleep no matter how good the book) and that indie publishing was similarly big. This meant that my first attempts at publishing were along traditional lines, searching for an agent. But that search left me feeling deeply dissatisfied. After doing some more research, and contemplating the nature of the first book I wanted to publish, I decided to try the indie route.

In studying indie publishing, I'd come across Dean Wesley Smith's blog, and much of what he wrote made sense to me. Things like how the best marketing tool is to publish the next book. Focus on building your backlist rather than trying to make a killing with your first novel. Have a high quality product – this means professional-looking covers, good proofreading, good copywriting. I didn't expect to make an immediate splash based on these principles, but I hoped over time to build a following and have a small measure of success.

I published my first book, *Emissary*, on January 2, 2015, and saw exactly what I expected to see – not many sales. I was fine with this; at this point I had ten novels at varying stages of readiness for publication, and I anticipated putting out a new book every couple of months. Which I did, in February (*The Smoke-Scented Girl*) and June (*Servant of the Crown*). I kept writing and learning and I practiced patience.

So far, this isn't a terribly exciting story, is it? Aspiring author overcomes mental illness and plugs away at writing, and over the years makes good. But that's not where the story goes from here. Because in July 2015, my third book, *Servant of the Crown*, the third book I'd ever written, went viral.

To this day, I have no idea what happened.

There had been a handful of sales, and some interesting online mentions; one website I had never heard of promoted the book by assembling a fashion collection – dresses, shoes, jewelry – based on the cover model. I only know that there was a day when I checked my sales and saw the total had gone from five to over fifty. That was the first day. I thought it was a fluke, but the sales kept climbing. The book's sales rank skyrocketed. People I'd never heard of told me they'd seen it promoted on Amazon. Other people showed up at conventions saying they'd bought the e-book and were there others?

It was stunning. It was terrifying. Because the one thing I hadn't prepared for was success.

It sounds like bragging, doesn't it? Everyone dreams of success like this, and because it's a dream, we think of it as unalloyed joy if the dream comes knocking on our door. But think of the authors whose first novels sell millions, and whose second novels are a disappointment. And then there's no third novel. This pattern makes the author money, but it does not make them a career. And I wanted a career.

As nice as it was to have success, I didn't know what to do with it. I had a plan, a plan that included having a ton of other books to point people at when they wanted more. Only I had exactly three books, one of which didn't have a great cover, none of which were like the other two. *Servant* had two sequels waiting to be published and I didn't dare rush either of them out the door, even to meet demand. I didn't know how to leverage the third book's popularity at all to benefit the others. I spent about a month flailing around feeling lost – happy, stunned, but lost.

Then I settled down to rework the plan. The first thing I did was come to terms with the fact that this success came way too early in my career for it to benefit me the way it would someone with ten or fifty books under her belt. There was no sense whining about that problem. So I needed to look at it differently.

I advanced production on the sequels *Rider of the Crown* and *Agent of the Crown*, though I was certain they would not satisfy a good chunk of the readership because they, like my other books, weren't anything like *Servant*. I built my newsletter base and sent out more regular updates. I saved as much of my income – I thought of it as a windfall, really – as I could and put the rest back into my career. I took advantage of as many marketing opportunities as I could handle, which wasn't many – at that point, the book was selling itself. I formed relationships with reviewers who could promote my next books. And, above all, I kept writing.

*

Continuing to write is the most important thing I did. Even the hottest books eventually decline in sales and popularity, and if you're counting on your income from your hot commodity continuing steady, you're bound to be disappointed. I believed – still believe – the best way to a long-term career is publishing regularly and consistently. What that means in practical terms will be different for each writer, but the core concept is the same.

All through the months of watching those sales rise, I kept writing and I kept publishing. I learned more lessons, some of them painfully hard – the story of my relationship with the mid-size press that published my other surprisingly successful book, *Burning Bright*, is a whole different essay twice the length of this one. I kept one eye on how *Servant* was doing. I wrote more books. And I eventually came to terms with success, just in time for sales to dwindle eight or nine months after that first amazing leap.

Seeing those sales drop was discouraging, I'll admit. But it would have been far more discouraging if I hadn't expected it to happen. Online advice from writers such as Kristine Kathryn Rusch told me that I wasn't the only one who'd ever had this problem – that publishing goes in cycles, and there are slumps as well as peaks. Because I knew it was coming, because I knew it was a natural part of the publication process, I wasn't blindsided by a sudden drop in income. I'd been careful not to plan my finances around those sales, so I didn't suddenly find myself in debt. I had enough to run my business – and being an indie author is definitely a business – with some extra set aside.

And I wasn't back where I'd started. I had a following. I was making money – not astronomical figures, but a decent income. People looked forward to my books, something more personally satisfying than the decent income. (No, I'm not saying I would be okay if all I ever got from book sales was acclaim. Never devalue your work by saying you'd do it for free. But as nice as money is, it's not at all the same as meeting someone who loves your work so much that meeting you strikes her speechless.) Six books in, I had the beginnings of the career I wanted. I was back on track after a spectacularly exciting detour.

I still had a lot to learn. I was and remain remarkably bad at marketing, something I'm sure would boost my career now that I have enough books to make it truly effective. My decision to pursue a hybrid career with the aforementioned mid-size publisher looked smart right up until the publisher started falling apart and I had to extricate five of my books from them. I experimented with form, I experimented with release strategies, and I had some successes as well as some failures. (It turned out releasing a trilogy all at once just made readers tired.)

But this is the thing that matters: *I never stopped pressing forward.* It would have been so easy, during those best-selling days, to ride the wave. It also would have been fatal to my career. As I've said, my long-term plan was to maintain a career, not to count on another success coming out of nowhere.

I think a lot of people, beginning and even more seasoned authors included, look at publishing as something where anything but an immediate and unqualified payout means failure. But in the indie world, that's really not how it works. There are thousands, maybe tens of thousands, maybe more, of authors who don't make a huge splash immediately. And yet so many of them are what traditional publishing would call mid-list authors: not bestsellers, but with quiet and loyal followings, and if they're indies, they're probably making a reasonable income. It is so much easier to become one of these authors than to base your success on grabbing the golden ring. (*Easier*, not easy.)

There were a lot of points along my path where I could have said "Enough." After all, I had the success I wanted, but what if it never came again? Suppose that one fluke hit was all I would ever get?

Failure, however you want to define it, after success is embarrassing. I might have gone from being able to gush to interested friends about how well my book was doing to having to avoid certain people so I didn't have to admit I hadn't had any sales in weeks. It's tempting to pull the plug while you're hot so you don't have to face the long, slow slide into obscurity.

Or I could have defined success by the money I was making. That's an easy measure, and it's not at all hard to tie your self-worth to your bank balance. I could have given up on writing once it was clear the income stream was down to a trickle. After all, by a certain logic, there's no point putting effort into something that isn't making you any money. There are so many other careers out there, most of them more consistently lucrative.

But taking either of these approaches means having to say "I *was* a success." Past tense. Being successful, staying successful, means not giving up in the face of either failure or success.

*

Though this is not the career I imagined I would have, I've learned so much from these experiences. I started out as a raw newbie, so completely uninformed I didn't even know I didn't know things. Because of this, I did things I would never do now, like formatting a print book in Word or trying to sell a 130,000-word fantasy romance. While there are things writers don't do because they are genuinely terrible ideas, sometimes not knowing what's impossible is what delivers success. So I tell new writers, particularly the ones who are on the indie track: take chances. Try something impossible. You may fail spectacularly, but no one can predict where spectacular success comes from either, so why not let it be you?

I've also learned the wisdom of being in this for the long haul. So many would-be writers focus on making a splash immediately, and tie their personal definition of success to this. The truth is, the writers who are still around ten or fifteen years after publishing their first book are the ones who stuck it out through the early years of not many sales and little recognition. Writers just starting out need to decide how much they want success and whether they're willing to endure the lean years for the promise of a long-term career.

And I've seen proved repeatedly the truth that the best marketing strategy is to write and publish the next book. Readers who love one of an author's books will seek out others, and having others for them to find is key to long-term success. Some of the most satisfying reader contacts I've had have been with readers who tell me they read one of my books and immediately went out and bought all the others. If "all of the others" means ten or twenty-five or fifty or more books, that's good news for your bottom line.

But what matters most in dealing with success or failure is knowing what success looks like for you.

Is it money? Bestseller status? Awards? Great reviews? Personal contact with fans? Something else?

When I had my first big breakout, I still didn't know what I wanted, and I had to decide fast because how I reacted to that turn of events would be shaped by my definition of success. Choosing what you want out of a writing career and holding fast to that will bring that success faster – most importantly because you are not letting someone else define success for you. Writers who know what they want will also gain more satisfaction out of their writing careers than the ones who turn in the winds of current prevailing opinion.

I've seen great success, as defined by certain parameters. I've seen failure as defined by others. And in both cases, I've seen the need to have the courage to continue, to look beyond the moment to what lies ahead. Instant success is exciting, but for me it was no substitute for going on past the moment when that early success faded. Even now, years later, I look forward to continuing the journey.

Lesons learned:
- ✓ Be prepared for success as well as for failure

- ✓ Look at your writing career in the long term, not with an eye to instant success
- ✓ Figure out a personal definition of success and pursue that
- ✓ Write the next book – don't obsess over the last one

*

Melissa McShane is the author of more than twenty-five fantasy novels, including her breakout novel Servant of the Crown, *first in the* Crown of Tremontane *series; the bestselling, award-winning* Burning Bright, *first in the* Extraordinaries *series; and her most recent series,* Company of Strangers. *She lives in Utah with her husband, four children, a niece, four very needy cats, and a library that continues to grow out of control.*

Short and Sweet
John M. Floyd

I'm sort of an oddity in the literary world: I'm a short story writer. (Those who introduce me, though, have to put the pause and the hyphen in the right place. At six foot four, I'm not a *short* story-writer – I'm a *short-story* writer.) And it's not that I don't like novels, or poems, or nonfiction. I've written some of all three. I just have a special love for short stories. Maybe it's because I grew up watching those little half-hour anthology TV shows like *Twilight Zone* and *One Step Beyond* and *Alfred Hitchcock Presents*. They were tightly written and fast-moving and often had surprise endings, and that kind of thing appeals to me on the page the same way it once appealed to me on the small screen. There's just something enjoyable about reading – and writing – short fiction.

I. Ancient History
The strange thing is, I didn't start writing at an early age. I started in my forties, when I was working for IBM and traveling a lot, spending many hours alone in cars and airplanes and airports and hotels. During that time – the early- to mid-1990s – I began dreaming up these little stories, and when I found out how much fun that was I began writing them down, and within a year or so I had manuscripts everywhere, not only stacked in my home office but in desk and dresser drawers throughout our house. Finally my wife, usually a patient lady, said enough was enough. She pointed out that since my stories seemed to be multiplying like rabbits, maybe I should send some of them to the editors of magazines – in

other words, get them out of the house – and see if I could get them published.

I didn't like that idea. For one thing, I loved my stories, and wasn't eager to mail them off to someone who might *not* love them. No mother likes being told her baby's ugly, and no writer likes to find out his creation isn't the masterpiece he thought it was. A second reason was that I had no idea how to go about submitting a story to an editor. How was I supposed to know how to do that? But my wife, growing even less patient now, pointed down the street and said, "There's the library – you can learn how." So I did.

Since all this took place in the pre-Internet days, I dutifully found two books on the library shelves that I hoped would help me in my quest: one was about manuscript submission – it described in detail such unfamiliar things as fonts, margins, spacing, cover letters, etc. – and the other was *Novel & Short Story Writer's Market*, a Writer's Digest book that lists hundreds of publications, along with addresses and editors' names, that would consider unsolicited short-fiction submissions.

Armed with these two resources, I chose five of my completed stories, formatted them as instructed, mailed them out to five different magazine editors, and sat down to wait. I can't say exactly what responses I expected, but whatever it was, it wasn't what I got.

Incredibly, four of those first five submitted stores were accepted and published – and I thought *Whoa, wasn't this supposed to be hard? I'll just send out a zillion stories and make a zillion dollars.* That, of course, didn't happen. What did happen was, the next thirteen stories I submitted were rejected. Thirteen in a row. And although I didn't realize it then, it was one of the best things that could've happened to me. It taught me that getting a story accepted is *not* easy. To have a story accepted for publication, a particular editor has to like your particular story on that particular day, and those are long odds. In some ways, the process is like a roll of the dice.

But I had also learned that *I actually could do this.* Unlike so many beginning writers who, for whatever reason, take a long, long time to get published, I was somehow able to see positive results right away, and that validation gave me enough of a boost in confidence to keep going. I can't even imagine what it must feel like to submit dozens and dozens of manuscripts and receive nothing but rejections, one after the other. If that happened, almost anyone would begin suffering self-doubt, and plenty of it. I'll always be grateful for that early success, even if it was fleeting.

II. Rejection and Dejection

The fact is – and I wouldn't learn this until later – good stories get rejected every day. Granted, some stories are bad, and deserve a quick trip to the trash can – but some might just be about a topic that the editor doesn't like (all of us have pet peeves), or some might be a little too much like another story that was published last month in that same magazine, or some might've had the rotten luck to arrive on that editor's desk when she was having a particularly hard day. Editors are human, and because they're human they sometimes make poor decisions.

But that's the way it works, in this business. As a writer, you have to try and keep trying. Do the best you can on a story, submit it to what you think is the proper market, and see what happens. As I've often told my writing students, I can't guarantee your story will be published if you send it in – but I can guarantee it *won't* be published if you don't. I think the most important advice a writer can receive is *Don't quit*. No matter what happens and no matter how many rejections you get. As someone way smarter than I am once said, "There's a lot of attrition among writers... so don't attrit." Something else I heard long ago: "A professional writer is just an amateur writer who didn't give up."

III. Learning to Read and Write

Again, most of what I've written has been short stories, and specifically short mystery stories, but a lot of the things I've learned along the way apply to all kinds of writing, and certainly all kinds of fiction – novels, short stories, novellas, novelettes, vignettes, plays, screenplays, etc. I have come to believe that there are some things that all of us, as writers, should attempt to do.

One of them is to read as much as we possibly can, and not only in our preferred genres. Mystery writers should read literary works now and then, and literary authors should read mysteries. Fiction writers should read nonfiction occasionally, and vice versa. I try to pick up a science fiction novel once in a while, or a fantasy story, or a Western, or a biography, or a book of poetry. We can all learn from that kind of thing; it's almost impossible not to. And I'm often surprised at just how much I enjoy it. One successful mystery writer I know says he makes it a point to read at least half a dozen classics each year – and he swears it's helped him to write better fiction in his own genre.

While we're talking about things all of us should do, another is to *write something every day*. And I'm not talking about emails or thank-you notes or church newsletters. Write something creative, either notes for a new story idea or additional pages for an ongoing project or a revision to a completed draft. If you think it'll help, set a quota of a certain number of words per day or pages per week. Personally, I don't set quotas for myself – I think that would make writing too much like work – but I do try to put something on paper or on my hard drive, or at least think through a plot in preparation for later writing, every single day. If you don't do that, and if you don't feel compelled to do that, well, you might want to reconsider this whole decision to be a writer. Writers enjoy writing, and they do a lot of it.

At the risk of using too many old sayings, I'll use one more here: The best way to be a writer is to read a lot and write a lot. Practice, at almost anything, makes us better.

IV. Style Points

This is probably a good time to say something about the writing itself – and specifically about *style*. Style is a term for the nuts and bolts of writing: grammar, punctuation, spelling, capitalization, word choice, word usage, sentence structure, paragraph structure, and so on. I won't go into exhaustive detail, but if you want to be a writer you must be willing to learn – or re-learn – all those rules about commas and apostrophes, etc., that we supposedly covered in high-school English classes. Yes, it's dry – but it's necessary.

In the old days, editors and publishers and agents tended not to put great emphasis on this kind of thing, in the manuscripts they received. If the story or novel contained grammar mistakes or misspellings or punctuation errors but it still showed promise, well, they figured they could whip it into shape. That doesn't happen anymore. The Powers That Be now expect your submission to be as error-free and print-ready as possible. If it's not, they'll just reject it and go on to the next manuscript in the stack, looking for one that *is* error-free and print-ready.

The good news is that once you learn the rules of style, you will then be able to break those rules when it's best for the story. I do urge you to cut back on those tiresome adjectives and adverbs and exclamation points – and for God's sake learn the difference between its and it's – but contrary to what most English professors seem to think, you as a fiction writer *can* occasionally splice commas, fragment sentences, split infinitives, and start sentences with conjunctions – and feel no guilt. The late Elmore Leonard once said, "I can't allow what we learned in English Composition to disrupt the sound and rhythm of the narrative." If it sounds right and works well for the story, it's probably okay. Do it and don't look back.

But knowing these rules, and breaking them when it's advisable, isn't enough in itself to produce a great story. You'll also need to create interesting characters and settings, put together a compelling plot, write believable dialogue, and choose the correct point of view through which your tale can be told. On top of all that, you must fashion an effective beginning, a middle that holds the reader's interest, and a satisfying (not necessarily a happy, but a satisfying) ending.

How do you learn how to do that? Read good stories and novels. In fact, read a bad story or novel now and then, just to see how it *shouldn't* be done. And work hard on your dialogue. Some editors/publishers/agents have said they often page ahead to the first passage of dialogue in a submission, read that, and only then – if it works – do they back up and start at the beginning. It's that important. (Very briefly, here are some tips to writing effective dialogue: (1) listen to the way people really talk, (2) read authors who write great dialogue, and (3) read your own dialogue out loud, to catch mistakes.)

What are some worthwhile books on the subject of style? A short list: *Self-Editing for Fiction Writers* by Renni Browne and Dave King; *The First Five Pages* by Noah Lukeman; *Dreyer's English* by

Benjamin Dreyer; the last half of *On Writing* by Stephen King; and, of course, *The Elements of Style* by William Strunk, Jr.

V. Increasing the Odds

Another thing that's good to know, if we're focusing on short stories, is that there are three things that writers can do, right off the bat, to help their chances of selling a story.

One goes back to what I said in the previous section: *include plenty of dialogue.* I of course understand that not every story lends itself to a lot of dialogue. I've written and sold a few that have no dialogue at all. But it's a fact that if you write two stories of the same quality and one of those two stories incorporates a lot of dialogue, it will be easier to sell.

The second thing is to *include humor.* This doesn't have to be laugh-out-loud humor; it can be funny banter between two characters, or understated irony, or having one character who doesn't take himself too seriously. Once again, not all stories lend themselves to this, but most do. Even otherwise serious stories. The same observation applies, here: if you have two stories of equal quality and one includes humor, that story will be easier to sell than the other.

The third and final thing a writer can do in a short story is to *make it shorter rather than longer.* It's not always possible; my favorite story of my own runs around ten thousand words, and if it were any shorter I don't think it would've worked. But once again – and you know what I'm going to say, here – if you have two stories of the same quality and one is ten thousand words and one is two thousand words, the shorter story will be easier to sell. I promise.

VI. Facts in Fiction

A quick word about researching stories. I usually find it necessary, unless I'm writing about myself or my family or my job or my hobbies or my hometown, to at least do some research to make sure I don't make a factual error of some kind. There are several ways to find out things you might be unsure about: (1) look it up, (2) ask someone who knows, or (3) go wherever you need to go yourself, and see it all firsthand.

Number one is easy as long as I remember that not everything I find on the Internet is true; number two is always effective, especially if I ask a professional in whatever field I need help with; and number three is appropriate if I'm writing about people or places within easy driving distance. I once wrote a story set in a nearby town, and before I started writing I spent an entire afternoon there, walking the streets my characters would walk and taking note not only of the sights but of the sounds, smells, etc. I think that helped me write a more realistic and more believable story.

It's also a good idea to remember that once I've done all this research, it can be extremely tempting to put too much of it into my story. Too much information, about anything, can bog a story down and bore the reader. A good trick is to include *only* those facts that I myself found fascinating. If I do that, chances are my readers will find them fascinating as well. I don't even like to describe in great detail what my characters or settings look like, or what my characters are wearing. Some things are best left to the imagination of the reader.

VII. Preparing to Launch

Okay, let's say I've done all that. I've done my research, put together what I hope is a readable story, written it with an eye toward flow and tightness and a solid style, and then rewritten and edited and polished it until I'm satisfied that it's as shiny as I can make it. Am I ready to send it out to a market? Not quite. It's now usually a good idea to let the story sit there and stew in its juices for a few days, maybe even a week or two, and then take another look at it with a fresh eye.

I say this because I know from experience that I will almost always find things after that cooling-off period that I failed to see before. It might be something major (structure, pacing, characters, plot, POV) or something minor, like style errors or typos – but that wait-time usually pays off. NOTE: This is hard to do, especially for me. When I finish a story, I want to get it out to an editor, and soon. But I've learned to be patient, on this. I let it rest awhile before dispatching it on its mission.

Now that that's done, and I've re-read the story and made those late corrections, I probably *am* ready to send my baby out into the world. But there are also a few things on the marketing side that we need to talk about.

First, I have learned not to pay ANYone ANYthing to consider or publish my work. I'm a firm believer that money should flow *toward* the writer, instead of the other way around. If my writing is good enough, whoever accepts my writing project should be paying *me*.

If I'm producing short stories, which is usually the case, I don't pay reading fees or "processing" fees. If a market's submission guidelines say it charges these fees, I find a market that doesn't – there are plenty of them out there.

If you're sending a novel to an agent, don't pay that agent a dime. Not even copying fees or postage fees for manuscripts he or she might send to publishers. Any money paid to your agent should be taken out of the money he or she makes for you via the sale of your writing. In that sense, it's like the fees charged by personal-injury lawyers: they only collect if you do. If *you* get nothing *they* get nothing.

VIII. Submission Control

As for the submission itself, I always craft a cover letter (if a short story) or a query letter (if a novel proposal) to accompany the submission. I make that letter – or that email, if you're submitting electronically – short, I address it to the correct recipient, and I leave out anything not relevant to the submission.

When I type the salutation, my rule has always been to use the editor's last name along with a Mr. or Ms., at least until he or she responds with only a first name or addresses me by my first name. After one of those two things happens, we're on a first-name basis from that point forward. (The publishing industry, you will find, is sort of a laid-back operation anyway.) And if an editor's first name is Pat or Lee or Lynn or something that could indicate either a man or woman, I leave off the Mr. or Ms. and type the whole name – Dear Pat Johnson – in the salutation. Better to appear stiff than to get it wrong.

Once the submission is sent, usually via email these days, or via the submission facility on a market's website, I try to completely forget about it until I hear back from the editor. I don't worry about it, I don't read it again, I don't even think about it. I certainly don't go back to my copy of the story and fiddle with it in the meantime, because if it happens to get accepted the editors sometime need you to re-send them an original copy of the story, and I don't want to have already made changes to the version they accepted.

And it probably goes without saying that if I don't receive an acceptance or a rejection after several months – usually three, unless otherwise specified in the guidelines – I send a polite inquiry email to check on the status of my submission. If I still fail to hear anything back from them after another wait, I send them a note informing them that I'm withdrawing that story from consideration, and keep a copy of that withdrawal letter.

One of the advantages of selling a short story, rather than a novel or a book-length piece of nonfiction, is that I can re-sell that story over and over again to other markets, as long as I haven't signed away "all rights" to the story. Most magazines and anthologies acquire "first rights," or FNASR (First North American serial rights), which means they get to publish that piece for the first time, before anyone else; afterward any publication buying that story would acquire only "second rights" or "reprint rights." And be aware that a writer automatically owns the copyright to his story once he has created it, and in order to lose that copyright he would have to sign it away in a contract.

Something else I think is smart, if you're writing short fiction, is to regularly submit stories to the big, prestigious markets. I'm not saying you should target *only* those – that would be setting yourself up for failure – but you also shouldn't ignore them and you shouldn't think you're not yet "good enough."

If you've studied the larger markets and read a few stories featured by those you'd like to submit to, and if you've created a story that you believe in, take a deep breath and send it to them. They might be big, but they also have a business to run, and that business involves providing quality stories to their readers. Sure, they probably publish mostly established writers; but they also need to find new writers as well, and sometimes lightning does strike. That's the way I got my first story in *Alfred Hitchcock Mystery Magazine*, back in 1995. I wasn't a big name and they certainly didn't know me. I just happened to send them a story that caught their attention.

IX. War Stories

In the twenty-five years that I've been writing for publication, several things have happened that, although they seemed strange at the time, have taught me valuable lessons.

One was a call I received back in 1999, not long after I submitted my first story to *The Strand Magazine*, a mystery magazine once famous for having published the likes of Conan Doyle and Agatha Christie. *Strand* editor Andrew Gulli phoned me, introduced himself, and said, "We like the story you sent us, John, but some of the folks on my staff are unfamiliar with the poison you used to dispatch one of the characters. Where did you find out about that poison?" (What had happened was, I couldn't find a real poison that worked the way I wanted it to work in the story, so I invented one, one that I'd said was made from the fluid of the oscolio blossoms of eastern Africa. There is, so far as I know, no such thing as an oscolio blossom, in eastern Africa or anywhere else.)

Suddenly nervous and seeing my possibility of a big sale slip-sliding away, I held my breath and told him the truth: "I made it up." There was a long, long pause on the line, and finally he said, "Okay." We then exchanged some more pleasantries and said our goodbyes, the story was published, and it was later listed in the back of *The Best American Mystery Stories 2000* as one of the top fifty mysteries of the year.

What did I learn from this? I learned that if something in your story's plot doesn't work, and if you've studied it and studied it and you've been unable to come up with anything that does work... it's sometimes okay to make something up, and run with it. Just be sure to make it sound believable.

On another occasion, a story popped into my mind while driving back from running errands a few miles away. I thought about the plot all the way home, and by the time I parked in our driveway the story, a really short one, was fully formed in my head. I rushed inside, typed it into the computer as fast as I could, spent a while rewriting it, and saved the final version.

As I mentioned earlier, it's always a good thing to let your stories sit awhile and cool off before submitting them, and I usually try to do that, but I was excited about this one and truly felt it was ready for prime time. I Googled a few markets, found a new one in the UK that I thought my story might fit, and emailed the story off to that editor, right then and there. Afterward, my wife and I sat down to supper.

Just as we'd finished, I heard a ding from my computer in the other room. I checked it and found an emailed reply from the editor I'd sent the story to, in London; he'd been working late and said he had seen my story come in. He also said he'd read it, he liked it, and he wanted to publish it. A contract was included in the email, which I printed, signed, scanned, and emailed back to him – and as a result, for the first and probably the last time in my life, I dreamed up a story and sold it within three hours, total. I'm not saying this will ever happen again – it probably shouldn't have happened at all – but in this electronic age, that kind of thing *can* happen. It is at least possible.

The last incident I'll mention occurred several years ago in a Kroger supermarket near our home. I was in the checkout line and was waiting to buy two copies of *Woman's World* magazine – one for my mother and one for my sister – because I had a mystery story in the current issue. When the longfaced and long-suffering cashier finally turned to me and my purchases, she looked tiredly at the two magazines, looked at me, and said, "You have two of these." I nodded and said, "I know." She sighed and said, "But you have two copies of the *same issue*." This time I stood up straight, gave her my highest-wattage smile, and said, "I know. Actually… I have a story in this issue."

There was a long silence while she stared at me and I stared at her and I checked my pockets to make sure I had a pen in case she wanted my autograph. At last, in a profoundly bored voice, she said, "That'll be four dollars and twenty cents." She didn't care a whit who I was or whether I had a story in the magazine. It was a good lesson for me: Authors shouldn't ever get too cocky about their accomplishments. We're not such a big deal after all.

X. Wrapup

In summary, and to recap a bit, here are half a dozen things I've learned in my quarter century of writing that I think might be helpful to other writers to remember:

1. Don't give up.
2. Read as much as possible, and write something, at least in your head, every day.
3. Learn the rules of grammar and style and then break them if you need to.
4. Let your finished stories "cool off" for a while before submitting them.
5. Never pay anyone to consider or publish your work.
6. Submit regularly to the big markets.

And, above everything else, have a good time with all this. Try to make everything you write as perfect as it can be, but don't take yourself too seriously. You're not building a rocket to Jupiter, ending famine in third-world nations, or discovering the cure to cancer. You're writing stories, primarily for entertainment.

Is it hard work, writing fiction? Sure it is. Any writer will tell you that. But I've never had more fun, and God willing, I'll never stop.

I wish you the very best in all your writing endeavors.

*

John M. Floyd's work has appeared in more than 250 different publications, including Alfred Hitchcock Mystery Magazine, Ellery Queen Mystery Magazine, The Strand Magazine, The Saturday Evening Post, *and two editions of* The Best American Mystery Stories. *A former Air Force captain and IBM systems engineer, John is also an Edgar Award nominee, a three-time Derringer Award winner, a three-time Pushcart Prize nominee, and last year's recipient of the Edward D. Hoch Memorial Golden Derringer Award for lifetime achievement. His seventh book,* The Barrens, *was released in fall 2018. John and his wife Carolyn live in Mississippi.*

Giving Up on Your Dreams
David H. Hendrickson

My passion for writing began with a friend lending me a short story collection by Harlan Ellison. Up until then, it hadn't even occurred to me.

I'd always been a math-and-sciences guy in high school, and I'd spent those years with the tunnel-vision goal of getting into the Massachusetts Institute of Technology. After I got my acceptance letter – early decision, no less – I put about a half-second of thought into my future and decided I'd major in Electrical Engineering so I could design my own stereo system.

Yup. So I could design my own stereo system. That was my plan for the future.

Once I arrived at MIT, however, a much different reality hit me. Actually, it bashed me over the head like a baseball bat. Crashing instead through my life's front door was the most mind-numbing, soul-crushing mathematics I'd ever encountered.

In course after course.

All thoughts of listening to music on a stereo system I'd designed got tossed unceremoniously out the window.

I don't hate math. In high school, I'd been co-captain of the math team. I'd thought algebra was fun and geometry pretty good. By the time the standard progression had moved to trigonometry and calculus, however, math had become drudgery. A necessary evil. I could appreciate their importance, but I found no fun in trig and calc.

At MIT, the next step led over the cliff edge of resigned acceptance into a deep, dark chasm of pure misery. Differential equations (*diffy-q's* in the parlance). Diffy-q's were a hundred times worse than the mathematics I had considered drudgery. A thousand times worse. A million.

I *loathed* differential equations. But they were an integral part of every engineering and math course, save Intro to Computer Programming, which used something called *lambda calculus* to suck the life out of that topic, too. Only a Music History course provided a respite from these assaults, and I was halfway prepared for that professor to use diffy-q's to explain the wonder of Bach's *Brandenburg Concerto No. 2*.

I hated virtually everything about MIT and what I was studying. What I had considered my life's goal – to get into MIT and then somehow survive it, since I had known from the start that everyone else would most certainly be smarter than I was – had become a nightmare. I couldn't conceive of spending the rest of my life working on differential equations.

On top of that, I was working a few weeknights and Saturdays as a telemarketer for Sears Roebuck. If you bought any kind of appliance at Sears, I called to sell you a maintenance agreement that would cover all repairs and an annual checkup. And if you'd already bought a maintenance agreement at the store, I called to "up-sell" you additional years.

Yes, I was that guy. A creature below cockroaches. A telemarketer.

This made my work-school misery complete. Other than having found the most wonderful woman in the world (admittedly, the most important caveat possible), my life was a mess.

I was ripe for the plucking.

A friend at that part-time job always had a paperback book tucked in his back pocket. He also had a reputation for long bathroom breaks. It wasn't hard to put two and two together. The guy loved to read even to the point of skirting the precipice of getting fired.

One day, he lent me Harlan Ellison's short story collection *The Beast That Shouted Love at the Heart of the World*. It changed my life forever. I read the title story, the first one in the book, and it hit me square between the eyeballs. Took my breath away. Poleaxed me.

This was what I wanted to do with my life! I didn't understand what the heck Ellison was doing with this very experimental story, but oh my God, I wanted to do it, too! The next day, I took out of sheet of paper and began to scribble the first couple paragraphs of my first story. To steal a line from Ellison himself, it felt like lightning was shooting out of my fingertips.

This was absolutely what I wanted to do with my life!

It was horrible, of course. I had previously shown not even a hint of interest in writing "that fiction stuff." I had none of the skills, none of the knowledge, not even the foundation of having read a lot of fiction myself. When I'd gone to the library, I'd checked out *The Boy Scientist* and incomprehensible books about neutrinos because they were presumably pieces to the puzzle that would get me into the Promised Land of MIT and the sure-to-be bright future that would follow.

So those first few paragraphs were predictably dreadful. When someone came up from behind me and asked, "What're you writing?" I dove on that sheet of paper, covering it up as if it were a grenade about to go off. I couldn't let anyone see the humiliating words I'd written.

But that didn't change the dizzying, intoxicating power of *creating something* that flooded over me. Yes, this was undoubtedly what I wanted to do with my life.

Unfortunately, there was that minor little problem of being horrible at it – other than that, Mrs. Lincoln, how did you like the play? Unlike a twelve-year-old who finds writing and in blissful ignorance of his ineptitude creates story after story, getting better while never being confronted by his lack of skills, I was old enough to know I was awful. I could look at Ellison's stories, and then look at my own pathetic attempts, and see they were universes apart. They had nothing in common.

Nothing.

I also had an extreme brain imbalance. We all have a creative side of our brains and an analytical side. My analytical side was powerful, developed – overdeveloped, in fact – by a lifetime's focus on math and science, analyzing everything from algebraic word problems to debugging computer programs. My analytical brain's cold, objective evaluation of my laughable writing attempts told my malnourished, emaciated creative brain that I had no talent and there was no hope of ever acquiring any.

When I wrote, my analytical brain would point to a paragraph I'd just written and slam on the brakes. Scoffing, it would tell me to fix this word and that word, then point me to the thesaurus for an alternate choice. I needed to rewrite the entire sentence. No, rewrite the entire paragraph.

Forget about trying to tell a story, it said. Fix every last detail. Fix this. Fix that. No detail is too small.

Don't try to tell a *new* story, it told me, and then went on to rub salt into the wound. Your story ideas are dumb. Any new idea you come up with will be dumb so don't bother. Instead, try to rewrite that steaming mound of crap called your last story.

You really do suck, it laughed – it seemed to like kicking me when I was down – do you really think anyone will ever want to read this crap? Do you really *want* anyone to read it? It's embarrassing. Do you realize how awful you are? You're a fraud, don't you know?

A *real* writer starts writing at an early age, it said, shaking its head in dismay. A *real* writer doesn't substitute writing as a life's goal for one that goes horribly sour. A *real* writer loves writing from the start.

My creative brain had no chance.

Writing in that era before electronic publishing also provided no feedback mechanism to let the writer know he was making progress. If you're a golfer, you can see your scores go down. If you're a salesperson, you see your commissions increase. If you play competitive chess, you see wins and draws replace losses, and your rating rises. But with writing, until you're close to the Promised Land of actually selling your work, you send stories out and they come back with a form letter rejection.

It's hard to maintain belief that you'll ever sell a thing.

And if your analytical brain – the brain you trust because even after the debacle of MIT, it's putting food on your table as a software engineer – if it tells you that you suck, you will always suck, and you are wasting your precious time, it's hard to argue. Especially when those form letter rejections keep adding exclamation points to what your analytical brain is already telling you...

*

Sports writing kept me going. And then it held me back.

I've been a sports fan all my life. It's baked into my DNA. I try to set limits on how much time I put into it (and invest any saved time into writing), but I could no more entirely remove sports from my life than I could willingly sever every last appendage from my body.

After the "Dick and Jane" books and their successors, I continued to teach myself to read by poring over the sports pages of the *Portland Press Herald,* the newspaper of record in southern Maine. Eventually, I was squabbling with my brothers over who got to read the sports section first. At one point, two of us kept getting up five minutes earlier than the previous day, morning after morning, so we could stand first in line by the front door and wait for the paper boy.

Baked into my DNA.

At the age of seven or eight, watching football on a small black-and-white TV, I became enthralled by an outstanding Princeton running back by the utterly awesome name of Cosmo Iacavazzi (pronounced *Yahk-a-vah-zee*). I couldn't repeat that name often enough.

Cosmo Iacavazzi. Cosmo Iacavazzi. Cosmo Iacavazzi. *(Even now as I type it, I'm smiling like a fool.)*

I was smitten. Smitten to the point that almost a decade later, Princeton was my number two school of choice, behind only MIT. All because a running back named Cosmo Iacavazzi had caught my eye.

I kid you not.

I was a nitwit, but a sport-crazed nitwit.

Years later, college hockey was added to the repertoire when my son, Ryan, began his life-long obsession with hockey. I had followed college hockey from a distance, but didn't dive deeply into it until he was a nine-year-old "Junior Chief," playing in the same arena as the UMass-Lowell Chiefs and going to almost all their games. Soon, I was firing off emails about UMass-Lowell hockey and its conference, Hockey East, on HOCKEY-L, an email discussion group used by fans in the days before websites.

When websites began to pop up, the founders of US College Hockey Online (uscho.com) who had seen my writing on HOCKEY-L, asked me to write for them.

An audience? An audience for my writing? Are you kidding me?

It wasn't fiction, but my short stories were going nowhere – I couldn't give them away – and every time I tried a novel, I'd quit in frustration as soon as I made the mistake of reading the god-awful dreck I'd written.

At USCHO, real live people would read my words! I was so starved for any kind of writing success at all, so desperate to reach readers of any kind, that this amounted to a flagon of artistic water offered to a writer dying of thirst.

I pounced. The USCHO founders warned that despite their professional aspirations, there'd be no pay in the early years while everyone tried to figure out how to make money on the Internet.

I didn't care. Money? I was far more desperate to have *some* reason to believe that someone, somewhere wanted to read my words.

The plan was for me to split responsibilities for covering Hockey East, one of the four major conferences. The 1995–1996 season had just ended, so we would write feature stories throughout the off-season as a means of ramping up interest (and our internal organization) for the start of the season in October.

Bubbling over with enthusiasm, I poured all my abilities – hopeful that I actually had some – into my first college hockey feature story. I submitted it, and held my breath.

Bull's-eye.

The powers that be decided they weren't going to waste my talents – *I had talent! I had talent!* – sharing the Hockey East beat with another writer. He was shuffled to another opening, and the Hockey East gig was all mine.

It was what my writer's soul so desperately needed – a reason to believe – but it also came at a steep price. I had a day job as a software engineer, I also taught Computer Science two or three nights a week at Boston University and UMass-Lowell, and most importantly, I had two teenagers that meant the world to me.

I wasn't going to sacrifice either my daughter, Nicole, or Ryan.

Something had to give. I decided that I would focus my writing energies on USCHO for this initial ramp-up off-season and then for the season itself. When the season ended, I'd flick the switch and return to writing short stories.

Sacrificing fiction writing for a year didn't feel like much of a sacrifice. After all, I was "giving up" something that didn't have any apparent worth. I hadn't sold a single story. The only one that had been accepted had been at a small magazine that paid in copies, and it had ceased publication before my story appeared. Besides, I wasn't giving up writing stories. I was just putting writing them on hold. A long-term plan of writing college hockey for six months, then short stories the next six, seemed the perfect compromise. Six off, six on.

I dove in that first year, and gave it all I had. When at season's end the USCHO staff gathered in a private room at the Frozen Four, the others pointed at me and began chanting, "MVP! MVP! MVP!"

It was a gratifying end to a successful first season. I might not be able to write fiction worth a lick, but I'd found a home in sports writing.

The fiction actually had to stay on the shelf another full year, though, because, intoxicated with my USCHO success – *success! Can you believe it?* – I decided to spend that first off-season writing a college hockey book. The short stories would have to wait.

The book project filled me with enthusiasm – *I was real writer!* – and I suspect subconsciously I was in no hurry to return to the persistent failure of my short stories. By summer's end, the book landed me an agent – something that seemed a big deal at the time, but I just shake my head over it now – but the book did not sell. It had a limited shelf life, and no publisher could have put it out in time for it to be anything more than the equivalent of year-old lettuce.

The following off-season, I finally did return to short stories. It had been a two-year absence, but it felt like twenty-two years. My sports writing had improved my style, but every fiction writing muscle had atrophied to nothing. Although it would take some time to realize it, sports writing had also improved my use of dialog. Each time I pared down a coach's rambling interview quotes into something effective that still sounded just like that coach and no one else, and identified him just as surely as a dialogue tag, I was learning lessons that would be important for my fiction.

I had also been learning how to make people laugh and sometimes cry. And I'd acquired a bit of a voice, albeit with no instincts on how to use it in fiction. I'd also learned that deadlines were not to be missed, and if that meant flipping the bird to that hyper-critical analytical voice, then so be it.

But the fiction-specific writing muscles were gone. I wasn't quite back to square one with those first scribbled paragraphs following the Ellison-fueled inspiration, but it sure felt close.

I swore never again to miss an off-season of writing fiction.

Even so, I soon found that writing fiction only in the off-season wasn't getting it done. Sticking religiously to six months on and six months off, year after year, wasn't going to lead me to any kind of fiction success.

I was at a crossroads.

Not to be immodest, but I'd become a big fish in the small pond of college hockey. I was the first part-timer and the first Internet writer to be honored with the Hockey East Media Award. I'd also shared in the Scarlet Quill Award. After my photo was added next to my columns, fans recognized me everywhere.

One night at a Northeastern University game, the student fans, mindful of the fact that in my column I'd picked their team to lose the game, began to chant in singsong unison, *"Daaa-ve! Daaa-ve! Dave Hendrickson! You suck!"*

It doesn't get much better than having the entire end of an arena chant that you suck.

Another year, I thought Boston College, usually a powerhouse, would be sunk because its goaltender had undergone hip surgery. I picked the Eagles to finish eighth in Hockey East. When they instead won the national championship, BC coach Jerry York teased me from the podium in his introductory remarks, saying, "Not bad for a team that Dave Hendrickson said was going to finish eighth in Hockey East."

Yet another year, before the start of a Hockey East championship semifinal, the LED Ribbon Banner that rings Boston Garden had a surprise for me. Where usually scores and advertisements appeared, moving round and round the display, this time a list of names was circling the arena. It was titled "The Legends of Hockey East." My name was one of them.

I tell these stories not to brag, but to illustrate the level of my accomplishments in college hockey. I'd become significant, and I was proud of my work. Damned proud!

But my fiction-writing dreams were slipping fast away.

In 2000, I had finally sold a humorous short story, "Yeah, But Can She Cook?" to an anthology called *Food and Other Enemies*. But I knew the editor, so that gave it a big asterisk in my mental tabulation of successes, even though I thought the story was pretty funny (and readers agreed). What's more, I kept the resulting twenty-five-dollar check for so long – perhaps becoming a bit like Gollum and struggling to part with it – that by the time I finally tried to cash it, the publisher had closed the checking account specific to that anthology. The check bounced. Technically, I was never paid.

So depending on how one maintains the scoreboard, I either had only one published short story* or none at all.

Definitely at a crossroads.

Someone suggested that I should stop torturing myself with fiction, where I seemed perpetually frustrated, and stick with what I was good at, namely sports writing. On the face of it, that was the only rational choice. It made no sense, based on the evidence to that point, to keep slamming my head against the wall of fiction. It promised to be awfully sweet if I would just stop.

What's more, I was getting painfully close to my fiftieth birthday. *The big five-oh.* And all I'd accomplished with my short stories was... if not nothing, zero, bupkis, then a microscopic number painfully close to that. A humiliating result best considered a skeleton in the closet. Slam that door, lock it, and throw the key away.

But fiction was my passion. It was why I had started writing in the first place. I might be getting close to fifty, but I wasn't dead yet.

*

Jeanne Cavelos and her *Odyssey Fantasy Writing Workshop* kept my fiction-writing hopes on life support. Kristine Kathryn Rusch and Dean Wesley Smith breathed life into it.

Facing that impending fiftieth birthday, I had a heart-to-heart talk with my wife, Brenda, truly the best person I have ever met, and the most astounding partner imaginable. Without her, you most assuredly would not be reading these words.

I had to find out for once and for all, I told her, if I was wasting my time. I didn't want to be haunted on my deathbed that I'd given up too soon on what (other than family) was my number-one passion. At the same time, though, how many years of humiliation did I need before I would accept the obvious, the near certainty that I simply *did... not... have... what... it... takes*?

I was almost fifty! Halfway dead!

I had to know.

I described for my wife a six-week, live-in workshop that a World Fantasy Award–winning editor named Jeanne Cavelos runs each summer. I could apply, see if I got in, and maybe...

Brenda told me in no uncertain terms to go for it. That meant no vacation for us. All to keep this flickering dream alive.

It was astounding support at a time that made no sense at all.

After I was accepted to Odyssey, I then had to convince my day-job boss to give me six consecutive weeks off close to the release of a key project. I didn't quite have to say that I would leave if he didn't grant it, but the implication was clear. This was not negotiable. And no, if something went wrong, I would not be able to ride to the rescue.

Approval was finally granted, albeit grudgingly, so long as I put all the pieces into place to avoid that key project from blowing up in all our faces. I did that as best I could, and headed off to Odyssey.

There, I worked with Jeanne and several guest writers, including Robert J. Sawyer, Christopher Golden, and Jeff VanderMeer. I bombarded every single one of them, multiple times, with one plea.

"Tell me if I'm wasting my time. Don't tell me what you think I want to hear. Tell me the truth. If I don't have what it takes, please put me out of my misery."

All of them responded that I was most definitely not wasting my time. I had things I needed to work on, but I was actually getting close to breaking through. I should keep going.

Armed with the mantra *The only one who can stop me is me,* I attacked fiction with a newfound ferocity. There would be no more six months on, six months off. I would write short stories all year long no matter how difficult. By this time, my daughter had graduated college and my son was about to enter his final year, so they were no longer around the house, needing their dad's constant attention. However, I still had the oft-demanding day job, teaching evenings during the Fall and Spring semesters, and writing for USCHO six months out of the year.

Didn't matter. That schedule wasn't going to stop me.

The only one who can stop me is me.

In the year following Odyssey, despite my schedule, I wrote fiction 365 out of 365 days.

The passion burned more than ever. I put into practice some of the technique lessons I'd learned at Odyssey. And when Dean Wesley Smith notified those of us on the Odyssey email list that he and Kris Rusch were offering an upcoming Master Class, I eagerly responded.

Dean asked about my writing, but he wasn't ready to accept me into the Master Class until I gave him the 365-for-365 statistic.

"That's the kind of writer we can work with," he said.

He gave me a challenge, the Story-a-Week challenge, that I now give to aspiring writers who ask for suggestions. Every week, you write a new story and send it out to a market. No rewriting an old story. No writing something and then shoving it into a drawer to fix later. A new story, start to finish. Send it out.

It's brilliant in its simplicity. For me, a guy who had gotten mired in the quicksand of rewriting a single story over and over and over until I was finally deathly sick of it, the challenge was a new lease on my creative life. When I got to Sunday night and sent the story out, I felt as though a burden had been lifted off my shoulders.

On Monday, I could start something new! This would be fun and exciting! I didn't have to guilt myself into thinking that I should grind the old one into something better – a fallacy since I'd seen plenty of times when revision number twenty was simply a 360-degree return to where I'd been with revision thirteen.

Each time I started and finished a story, I learned how to be a better storyteller. And I was having *lots* more fun.

By the time I attended Kris and Dean's Master Class, I was well on my way. Those two weeks – the toughest two weeks of my life – forced that cranky old analytical brain to give way to the creative brain. The cranky old fool didn't go easily, but it finally went down. No more driving with the brakes on.

*

When I first started writing all those years ago, I had three dreams. I dreamed that one day, one of my stories would receive a Best Story Award. I dreamed that one of them would be selected for a Year's Best anthology. And I dreamed that I would hold in my hands a collection of my own short stories.

Well, early in 2018 – *decades* after reading that first Harlan Ellison short story, twelve years after the Odyssey workshop, and nine years after Kris and Dean's Master Class – I received word that my story, "Death in the Serengeti," had been selected for *Best American Mystery Stories 2018*, my personal favorite Year's Best anthology, one which I've been buying for two decades.

A couple months later, I learned that two of my stories were finalists for the Derringer Award, presented annually by the Short Fiction Mystery Society. "Death in the Serengeti" was one of five finalists in the Best Long Story category; "The Kids Keep Coming" was one of five Best Short Story finalists. In May of that year, the Society announced that "Death in the Serengeti" had won. I was presented with the award that fall at the World Mystery Convention. And the most supportive wife in the universe was there with me to share it.

In that same year, I released my first short story collection, *Shimmers and Laughs: Eight Wildly Hilarious Tales.*

Three dreams fulfilled in one year. I'm glad I didn't quit when every piece of evidence suggested – no, *demanded* – that I'd be a fool if I didn't.

I've also been blessed with other dreams coming true. Dreams that I hadn't even dared to dream of, or that hadn't even occurred to me, way back when. I've released seven novels, including *Offside* and *Cracking the Ice,* which have been adopted for high school student required reading. I've stood in front of assemblies of those students, one of which had a section of them chanting the name of my book while the applause thundered over me.

And when that day seemingly couldn't get any better, I not only signed hundreds of copies of my book, I was asked to improvise for those students who'd forgotten their copy and experienced the rock-star moment of using a Sharpie to sign *students' arms*.

I kid you not.

All that for a guy who had wondered if he had any talent at all. A guy who had wondered if he was just wasting his time.

Do you think I'm glad I didn't give up too soon on my dreams?

Lesons learned:
- ✓ Don't give up on your dreams
- ✓ Find outlets for your writing to keep you going
- ✓ Learn from people who have been successful for a long time
- ✓ If writing is important to you, make it the priority it deserves
- ✓ Surround yourself with people who will support your dreams; ignore the voices that tell you to give up.

*

David H. Hendrickson has published seven novels, including Offside *and* Cracking the Ice, *which have been adopted for high school student required reading, as well as two short story collections, and two nonfiction books. His short fiction has appeared in* Best American Mystery Stories 2018, Ellery Queen's Mystery Magazine, Heart's Kiss, Pulphouse, *and numerous anthologies, including many issues of* Fiction River. *He is a multi-finalist for the Derringer Award, and his story* Death in the Serengeti *was honored with the 2018 Derringer Award for Best Long Story.*

Visit him online at www.hendricksonwriter.com

[Note: This essay first appeared in a different form as the introduction to David H. Hendrickson's short story collection Shimmers and Laughs: Eight Wildly Hilarious Tales.*]*

Erma and the Bag Lady
Tassie Kalas Haney

I saw the bag of my dreams at the Nutcracker Market in Houston one November. Shaped like a miniature typewriter, with rhinestone jewels for the keys, and *Once Upon a Time* scrolled across the top, the purse twinkled at me under the fluorescent lights.

The sales clerk had to pry it out of my hands to wrap it in tissue and place it in a shopping bag. "It's our last one." She noticed my tears. "You must really like typewriters."

Embarrassed, I wiped my eyes. "I have to have it." I whispered, "I want to be a writer one day."

I took my treasure home and displayed it on the fireplace mantle in my bedroom, where it gathered dust like a forgotten dream. *One day I'll use it*, I thought, even though it's impractical, something to be pulled out for special occasions. *One day, I'll be a writer.* But that was impractical, too. In the meantime, I kept my purse and my secret wish carefully hidden at home.

I'd spent most of my life a closet writer, hiding my thoughts and feelings in notebooks I kept private from the world. In elementary school, my mother bought me my first diary, complete with a lock and tiny gold key. *Keep out! Reading this may be dangerous to your health and mine, too,* I scrawled on the first page.

By the tine I reached high school, I'd graduated to writing in journals. I took my first journalism class, had feature articles published in the school newspaper, and basked in the glory of seeing my name in print. In college, a professor encouraged me to submit a humorous piece I had written about struggling to do the

Jane Fonda workout, which was the rage in the 80s. I was thrilled when the newspaper published it, complete with a photo of me sporting a perm and an author bio.

I loved the power my pen had to make people laugh.

*

As an adult, few people knew I belonged to a writing critique group. Years ago I shared one of my stories with the members. In my usual self-deprecating style, I read them, *Spin Cycle*, about the horror and humiliation of teaching my first spinning class.

The group howled with laughter at the description of the middle-aged woman sweating on a bike, wearing spandex in a room full of young, fit people, her varicose vein pulsing to the beat of *I Will Survive*. Whether they were laughing with me, or at me, didn't matter. They were laughing, and it warmed my heart.

The leader chuckled. "There's a workshop for humor writers." He tapped something on his laptop and showed me the screen.

The Erma Bombeck Writers' Workshop. A spark of excitement ignited in my heart. He scrolled down the page. *Dayton, Ohio.* My shoulders slumped. Recently divorced with three young children, traveling solo across the country was a work of fiction. I read the fine print at the bottom. *Sold out.*

Still, a tiny flame burned deep within me. I slipped the workshop into my mental *One Day* file.

Intrigued, I subscribed to the Erma newsletter and learned the workshop was only offered every two years, and sold out within hours. Disappointed, I placed that dream on my bookshelf next to my *Writer's Digest* where they both gathered dust.

In the meantime, my children graduated high school and college. One got married. I remarried. As I got older, I got bolder, and became determined to find a home for my writing.

Each month, I received a glossy neighborhood magazine in my mailbox, full of feature articles about the people in my community. Each month as I leafed through the colorful pages, I told myself I could have written these articles. I reached out to the editor three times by email asking for an opportunity to write for the publication, but never heard back.

Months passed.

In a last-ditch effort, I bought a black binder, stuffed it with samples of my writing, and marched into the magazine's office. I could see I'd interrupted a meeting, and considered making a dash for the exit before anyone saw me, but I took a deep breath, squared my shoulders, and stood at the reception desk, sweating, until someone came out to greet me and wrench the binder out of my hands.

To my amazement, a week later I received a phone call and my first assignment: to write an article about football moms, those women seen all over town sporting jerseys of their favorite high school teams. I soon discovered this type of writing was labor intensive. It required tracking down the subjects to be featured in the article, interviewing them, and creating a positive piece based on their quotes.

The goal of finally seeing my name in print motivated me to continue freelancing for the magazine. I loved meeting new people and helping them share their stories with the world. I met with musicians and models, artists and entrepreneurs. I tracked down prom moms and prodigies. I even interviewed a pageant queen, the daughter of the last man on the moon, and an American Ninja Warrior.

But while feature writing helped me reach my goal of being published and built my confidence as a writer, deep inside I still yearned to write fiction and get my first short story published.

For years I'd been entertaining my writing group with tales of what I knew best – growing up Greek, family, marriage, and motherhood. Inspired by the antics of my three children, I wrote openly about them, not bothering to change their names. Readers of all ages seemed to be able to relate to the mishaps and misadventures of my main character, a middle-aged woman juggling motherhood, divorce, and dating, struggling to gain her independence and become the strong, powerful woman she is destined to be.

The laughter of my critique group was rewarding, and though I valued their support and feedback, I wanted more – to find a home for my stories. I didn't feel like a writer if no one could read what I'd written.

I began searching for publishing opportunities and discovered the *Listen to Your Mother Show*, a series of live, on-stage readings across America. The Southeast Texas show was accepting submissions about motherhood and holding auditions in the area. On a whim and a prayer, I sent in my short story, *First Dance*, about a mother who drives her daughter and her date home with one eye on the road, and one eye on the backseat. I was invited to audition! The judges laughed as hard as my writing group had, and I was chosen to be in the show.

Getting the chance to perform a story I'd written to an auditorium full of people and hearing them laugh at all the right places was a dream come true. I didn't care whether people were laughing with me or at me. Their laughter was all the affirmation I needed, and it fueled my desire to write another funny story, and another. Through the experience I discovered the power of humor to connect the human spirit.

After that, I joined the Houston Writers Guild and became a member of a small weekly critique group. The talented, published writers in my group edit with eagle eyes and keep me motivated and accountable. They inspired me to begin attending HWG conferences which offered workshops on creativity, editing, publishing, and branding, and provide the invaluable opportunity to network with other local writers.

The guild also hosted free classes at local libraries where writers, agents and publishers taught their craft. I found a class on flash fiction, and attended along with a roomful of other hopeful writers. "We love humor," said the speaker, the president of a literary journal. "But it's very difficult to write."

He seemed to be talking directly to me. I accepted his challenge, and the next week submitted my only short, short story, *Lickety Split*, about my daughter being the lone member of her drill team who couldn't do the splits, and how this stretched us both to the limit. To my delight, the journal accepted my submission, and in a flash my first story was published!

I continued to submit my stories and as a result, began to collect rejection slips like others collect rare coins or stamps:

"Thank you for sending us your story. We appreciated the chance to read it. Although we feel it has literary merit, this piece is not for us..."

But these stamps of disapproval only helped me learn to cherish the rare successes, when a manuscript was magically accepted, and I'd float above the keyboard for days. I came to respect the rejections, to view them not as roadblocks, but as redirections, helpful guidelines to navigate me down the writing path I'd chosen. I even convinced myself not to take them personally. I compared the process to finding a beautiful dress at my favorite store, but when I tried it on, as lovely as it was on the hanger, it just didn't fit me. An entertaining story is a lot like an eye-catching dress – it's not one-size-fits-all. Not every reader can wear it, not every agent will send it down the runway. It's all about finding that perfect fit between writer and publisher – and that goes both ways.

When the guild hosted a contest for a travel-themed anthology, *Outside the Window-Tales of the World*, I took a chance and submitted two stories I had written about family vacations. In *Northern Heights*, a woman faces her greatest fear when her daughters shame her into going zip-lining. In *Juan, Two, Three*, a recently divorced single mom braves taking her children to Mexico, a trip that almost ends in ruins, until she realizes the best revenge for a broken heart is living a good life. I was thrilled when the HWG accepted *both* of my submissions for publication and awarded me an Honorary Mention for each story.

The best part of that honor was getting the opportunity to read a section of *Northern Heights* at the award ceremony and hearing the audience's laughter first hand.

*

Through it all, I never forgot about the Erma Bombeck seed my first critique group leader planted in my mind. Almost a decade had passed before the timing was right and everything fell into place like words on a page. I had been following her website for years and saw the workshop was accepting humorous submissions for an anthology on aging. On a whim, I dug out *Spin Cycle* and sent it in, then because I was aging, too, promptly forgot about it.

The day registration opened for the 2018 workshop, my fingers flew across my keyboard, and with a flying leap of faith, I clicked *submit.* And waited. My heart soared when the registration confirmation flashed across the screen, and I performed a victory dance in my study. My *one-day* was only four months away!

When I joined the Facebook page for attendees, and studied photos from past workshops, my courage crumbled. These women were writers, every one of them. They had books and blogs and bios. They had attitude and ambition. More than one wore a tiara on top of her pink hair. I would never fit in. I feared I'd be the oldest, most unfunny woman there.

The morning of my flight, I was wheeling my suitcase out of my bedroom and as an afterthought, grabbed my typewriter purse off the mantle and stuffed it into my carry-on.

Hours later, I stumbled into the University of Dayton Marriott, weary from travel. In my room, a downy king-sized bed beckoned me, and more than anything I wanted to disappear under the warm folds of the comforter. Room service would taste a lot better than an awkward dinner with strangers.

But, in honor of Erma, I mustered up my courage, hung my nametag around my neck and reapplied my lipstick. I pulled out my little typewriter purse. One drink at the bar, one pass through the bookstore, and I'd slip into the dining room and sit in a spot closest to the door. I could stash my sparkly purse under the table if it was out of place – and crawl down there with it if I was.

I ordered a cocktail, strolled by a table with Erma swag for sale and spotted copies of the anthology I'd submitted my story to months before. *Laugh Out Loud.* I drew in my breath. The cover was bright red, with laughing faces framing the title. I quickly turned to the table of contents and searched for my name. Then my heart sank. *40 Women Humorists Celebrate the Then and Now, Before They Forget.* They'd chosen forty women humorists… My silly spin cycle story by a barely published mom from Houston must have crashed and burned on the editing table. My typewriter purse sagged at my elbow.

I was thinking about skipping the banquet when a woman behind me tapped me on the shoulder. She had an engaging smile and a copy of *Laugh Out Loud* in the crook of her arm. "I love your handbag!" Her excited voice carried and soon a group gathered around, admiring my typewriter. "What a perfect purse for a writer!"

My bag glowed from the attention. Somehow, it had introduced me to women who were just my type. Although it was too small to hold much more than a few freshly printed business cards and my hotel key, it was growing on me. It held my heart and a whole lot of dreams.

The woman gestured to two writers beside her. "Want to sit with us at dinner?"

"Yes!" I smiled, grateful for the invitation.

We entered the ballroom, and sat down. As the waiters served us wine, my new friend leafed through the anthology. She checked out my nametag again. "Why didn't you tell us you were one of the authors in the book?" She pointed a polished fingernail at *Spin Cycle.*

I grabbed her book and turned to the table of contents. It was then I noticed it was divided into two sections, *Then* and *Now.* My story wasn't listed in the first part, but held a glorious place in the second.

My heart soared. Suddenly I was more than a middle-age mom with a Mac. I wasn't just full of wit. I was a *writer.* What a novel idea! Not only that, I was a *humorist.* It said so on the cover. And hearing someone say it out loud made me believe it could be true.

A new chapter of my life had begun.

At the end of the workshop, I didn't mind being left holding the bag. In fact, I carried my little typewriter home with pride.

*

As a new writer, I've learned lessons through trial and error that can help others beginning the journey towards publication. I find it helpful to read what I want to write and write what I want to read.

Reading essays and stories from my favorite authors is a great way to come up with fresh ideas. Once I have an idea, I put myself in the place of my character and ask, "What if?" Then I allow the story to answer that question. More importantly, I try not to self-edit my first draft, ignoring what my mother or husband might think of my story, at least until it's published.

And when there's the dreaded writer's block in the middle of the road, I detour around it, recognizing it could mean I'm still busy living the story I'm trying to tell. To combat it, I change topics or go somewhere else to write. If the writing well runs dry, I step out of my comfort zone for motivation. Taking a class, challenging myself with a new activity or traveling can get the keyboard clicking again.

And if my inbox is filled with more rejection than acceptance letters from publishers, I recover, resubmit and reach out to my readers in other ways, because I've found that being a writer takes more than aligning words on a page in a pleasing way, but being brave enough to offer up my heart and soul for dissection.

I've learned to start out by reaching out to smaller publications for recognition, to enter contests in my genre, and network with other writers through workshops and critique groups. I created an author's blog and a website to reach more readers, and started a writer's page on Facebook where I promote other writers through social media, and they in turn promote me. When I began treating my writing as a business, complete with branding and advertising, one line at a time, it began to grow.

New writers can benefit from the lessons I've learned at the keyboard:

- ✓ Be brave – your words will never see the light of day if you keep your masterpieces in the closet. Don't be afraid to share and submit your work.
- ✓ Write what you know – every story may have already been told, but not *your* story in *your* unique voice.
- ✓ Find a writing tribe – the right critique group will challenge you to reach your personal best, through constructive criticism. Be wary of groups who are too nice to be honest.
- ✓ Attend workshops and conferences – find one in your city or venture out to other parts of the world for publishing advice, marketing hints, and tips for improving your craft
- ✓ Be persistent – don't ignore the feedback you get through rejection, but don't stop submitting until you find the perfect fit for your work.

After years of pouring my thoughts onto the page, I've finally found my writing voice, and I'm not afraid to use it. No longer do I keep my words under lock and key, too shy to show the world.

Erma once said, "When I stand before God at the end of my life, I would hope that I would not have a single bit of talent left, and could say, 'I used everything you gave me.'"

I'd like to think she'd add, "Life is short. Buy the handbag. And never stop *purse-suing* your dream."

*

Tassie Kalas Haney is a member of the Houston Writers Guild, and has been published in The Ocotillo Review, *and* Laugh Out Loud, 40 Women Humorists Celebrate Then and Now..., Before We Forget, *an anthology that was named a finalist in the 2019 New Generation Indie Book Awards competition for humor. She has also won honorary mention for two short stories published in* Outside the Window – Tales of the World *and is currently working on a short story collection. Visit her at TassieTypes.com*

It Takes the Tenacity
to Persist

James A. Hunter

I never, *ever* expected to be a writer – and certainly not a full-time one who runs a small, thriving publishing company. If you had asked me even five years ago whether *this* would be my future, I would've called you crazy. Many of the writers and authors I've met and talked to since starting on this wonky journey have *always* known intuitively this is what they wanted: To sling ink and do the pen-monkey jig all while entertaining strangers with their musing and stories. Not me.

And yet...

Yet, here I am. Five years later, twenty-three full length novels under my belt, and nearly half a million books sold and counting.

It hasn't been an easy journey – it's been hard work, mountains of doubt, sleepless nights, and lots of gambles, yet... Here. I. Am. And boy have I learned some lessons along the way – little bits of publishing folklore that might help other wayward authors on their path to publication in whatever format that might take. So, as I walk y'all through my unlikely story, I hope to drop some of those hard-fought nuggets of wisdom gleaned along the way.

Okay, now back to the story.

I didn't always want to be a writer, and I never thought I'd be an author by vocation. I'd dabbled with writing on and off throughout high school – mostly short fic of the horror and fantasy variety – and fooled around with it a time or two during my stint in the Marine

Corps, but it was always as a hobby, more of an afterthought than a potential future. And even when I did start to take writing seriously enough to pen an actual novel, I sort of fell into publishing almost by accident and then proceeded to stumble my way blindly forward into becoming something of an indie publishing expert.

Which brings me to my very first piece of publishing expertise: *being clueless doesn't mean you're hopeless.*

Everyone starts somewhere, and being new to the game isn't some death sentence, though it feels like it at times. But remember this truth and hold it dear – everyone was new, once. No one starts out with all the answers, as some sort of master story teller who instinctively knows how to navigate the deep and ever-shifting waters of the publishing industry. But, when you read books by writing gurus or attend almost any of the writing conventions out there, it can be painfully easy to feel as though everyone knows more than you. It is easy to think you will forever be hopeless.

Not true, as I can testify first hand. Everyone was new, most people are lost in the sauce, and even those who seem to have it figured out, probably don't. We're all working through this thing together and if you are willing to learn and have the tenacity to persist long enough, you'll get the hang of things.

*

I started writing seriously in 2014 while my wife and I were living overseas in Bangkok, Thailand, as international aid workers. Thailand is a beautiful country, but one not without its issues; among those issues is that its challenging to get proper American television! Virtually overnight, Netflix, Amazon Prime, and YouTube had all vanished from my life along with both X-Box and Playstation. In one fell swoop, all the time-suck blackholes which had chewed up my time disappeared. *Poof! Gone.* With a tremendous void and a sudden abundance of free time (even while working full time and being a brand-new father), I started writing again.

And, truthfully, its incredible how much time you end up having by just eliminating television from your daily life. At the time, I didn't think I was writing at an exceptional quick rate, but I was doing it *consistently*, day in day out, and, in just under five months, I had myself a full-length Urban Fantasy novel that I felt pretty proud of. It was a hot mess, one which I had to polish and shine for the next five months, but by God I had a book. That moment, when I had a finished manuscript in my hands with the words *'The End'* boldly written at the bottom, was a life changer. Because not only had I accomplished this seemingly insurmountable task, but I'd done it *quickly.*

It was, dare I say it... Easy. Almost too easy.

But that's when I learned the second important lesson, which bears thinking about: *little actions daily, can create big changes when done over time.*

Writing a book, or more than one, is a daunting prospect, and rightfully so. It's a big, unwieldly endeavor that is messy and chaotic and filled with uncertainty. Many people give it a good go only to run out of steam and call it quits the second things get a little rough. That, or they find life intruding and eating into the time it takes to write, or research, or market, *or, or, or...* If, however, you break writing a book or any enormous task – be it finding a publisher, marketing your current book, hiring a voice actor, *literally whatever* – down into *little daily actions*, you can accomplish just about anything you want.

Over time, that is.

And for those who might say, *but that's exactly the problem. I just don't have the time to do it even though I really want to...* Well, I'd challenge you on that. I'd challenge you to examine your life and document how you actually use your time. Because, really, it doesn't have to be *a lot* of time. Maybe you wake up half an hour early, go to bed half an hour late, or cut out that one extra episode of *The Office* – which you've totally already watched five times. Block out a chunk of time *every single day* and pursue your goal. Write the next page, take that next course on marketing, send off those emails, or talk to those book bloggers. The important thing is you make the habit of doing it regularly, and treating that time as though it were sacred.

Which is exactly what I did.

I woke up every morning, worked for an hour, and hit the keyboard an hour again every night. Writing the book was only the first step, though. There I was, in Thailand, hopelessly mired in the perspective publishing bog, with my wife, my baby girl, and my shiny new manuscript. I didn't really know what I was supposed to do with it now that I had it, but I'd overcome the first hurdle. The next obstacle was to figure out how to move forward. Enter stage right. *The internet.* Since I was living overseas, I didn't have the option to do the convention circuit or talk with other writers who were in the same boat as me, so I turned to my only hope: *random strangers in online forums.*

Yay for research!!!

I used the time I'd previously dedicated to writing my book to study what I was supposed to do with my book. Turned out, there were lots of people with lots of different ideas about what the right next step was. Most of them didn't agree with one another and some of them seemed militantly dedicated to their way of doing things.

This, in turn, leads me to my third piece of advice: *most people – especially people on the internet – are full of crap and have no idea what they're talking about.*

I think this rule can also be broadly applied to both writers at conventions, dispensing sage advice, and *all* writing advice in general. As I am a person offering you sagely writing advice, you should be highly suspect of literally everything I'm telling you. It's probably lies. Or at least mostly lies. Or is it? You don't know because no one really knows anything. Which is why it is *vitally* important to consider many different sources (no matter how knowledgeable a person may seem) before you come to any sort of conclusion. Moreover, when someone tells you that they have *the truth* about publishing – especially if the truth comes with a price tag – it's probably best to walk away.

Thankfully, I followed the advice above, and after scouring the Google machine, I initially stumbled on something called *Traditional Publishing,* which seemed to be the most common way for homeless, orphaned manuscripts to find a home where they could mature and grow up to become *real* books with fancy covers and legions of fans. Or so we all hope. For several months I learned as much as I could about traditional publishing – or at least, as much as an outsider living in Thailand could learn – while crafting a meticulous query letter, synopsis, and researching potential agents.

After several months, however, I became frustrated with the process, which to me seemed incredibly slow and terribly inefficient. I had no aims to be a 'real author' and never dreamed it would be a job or career, so I started to dive more thoroughly into something else I'd stumbled across during my initial bout of research: indie publishing. Back into the research mines I went. I read every book and blog I could find, and though there seemed to be quite a bit of stigma associated with self-publishing I decided that was the route for me. Sure, it was likely my project would die, but it would die valiantly in the Wild West of Amazon Publishing instead of silently in some forgotten slush pile.

Which brings us to publishing lesson number four: *There is no one right way up Dream Mountain.*

That's right. Traditional publishing is awesome – for some people. Indie publishing is great too, for others. Neither way is all good, nor is either way all bad. They both have valid strengths and weakness. Traditional publishing is almost egregiously slow, while indie publishing is, at times, *too* fast; most successful indies publish, at minimum, four books a year. That's a whole lot of words. If you get a deal with a traditional publisher, your cut on royalties will be significantly less compared to self-publishing, but you also risk nothing but time with traditional. You might make more doing it yourself, but you might invest a lot of money and make nothing at all.

Like I said, there are many ways to the summit. Generally, anyone who tells you there is really only one way up is either woefully ignorant (*see piece of advice number three*), or they are disingenuous and trying to sell you something.

Having decided which path was right for me, I made a plan. And I decided that if I was going to do it, I was going to do it right – I've never been one for half-measures. I refused to cast my new-born book to the wolves without first giving it every fighting chance possible.

To do so, though, would be no easy task; I needed to find beta readers, an editor, a cover artist, and set up a marketing plan. And that? That all took time and, more critically, *money.* Money I didn't have. But my wife believed in me, and though we were living on a shoestring budget, we committed to saving up $1,500 over six months. It hurt to save that money, but there was no other path forward. So, we saved. We skipped meals out. We picked family activities that were free to do. We pinched every penny we could find. At the same time, I continued studying: finding artists, getting an editor, building my marketing plan, contacting book bloggers.

In what seemed like no time, I had become something of an accidental publishing expert and I'd transformed my book hobby into a full-fledged book business.

Which is my fifth piece of advice: *If you want this to be a business, you need to treat it like one.*

I know, I know. Money is tight. Saving is hard. You just want to put your book out into the world with that hand drawn cover, because hey *'don't judge a book by its cover,'* am I right?

No. No. You are wrong. Maybe you don't need to have a physical book with a physical cover, but you absolutely need snazzy, genre-appropriate, eye-catching art.

If you're writing and publishing for yourself with no intention of making money or treating this like a business, then go nuts and do whatever you want. But for the rest of you, you need to treat this like a business from the get-go, or you will likely never succeed. Indie publishing is not what it once was. It is now highly competitive with amazing books – books with compelling stories, great editing, and amazing cover art – coming out like clockwork. To be competitive and make money, your book needs to be as good or better than every other book out there, because guess what. Every other book out there *is* your competition. And not just my books, but Steven King's books and Lee Child's books and George R.R. Martin's books.

Save the money. Do the work. Put out a professional product – you owe it to your future readers to deliver the best possible novel you can. Anything less is a disservice to them and to yourself and the hard work you put in to making an amazing book.

*

Six months later I had a professionally edited book with a great cover and a solid plan for making sure my ideal readers knew my book existed. In January of 2015 I launched my first full-length novel under my own personal Imprint – Shadow Alley Press – and executed my plan with silent prayers and fingers crossed. I set the bar at a realistic level. I wanted to earn back my initial investment inside a one-year time frame – a lofty goal, but one I thought was realistic and reasonable. I'd done the leg work, put in the effort, and invested the time and money. Now, all that was left to do was roll the dice.

The book earned out in two weeks.

Inside three weeks, I started receiving my first fan-emails asking when book two was due to hit shelves. I hadn't even started book two, because I'd been so busy working the business side of things. I decided it was time to get back into the swing of writing. I outlined book two, dove back in, and managed to cut the writing time down to three months. Since I'd already done so much of the work for book one – I already had an editor, a cover artist, and a marketing strategy in place – that second book practically *flew* by. This time around I also had the money to fund the project right out of the gate by simply reinvesting the profits from book one directly into the next project.

That novel, *Cold Hearted*, came out in May of 2015. It too, earned out in its first weeks, and even better, book one was still selling. I hit book three even harder, applying the lessons I'd learned while cranking out the first two volumes; the process was even faster, more efficient, and more profitable. It still wasn't enough money to properly live from, but it was a huge step in the right direction and before long I found myself confronted with an unbelievable truth: I'd somehow, in my spare time, become a professional novelist.

*

When we transitioned back to the US from Thailand, neither my wife or I had any serious job prospects, but our publishing business was now a toddler and starting to take its first real steps. Jeanette, my wife, always had an entrepreneurial spirit, so in mid-2017 she came on board full time, taking over the business side of things so I could write more, and write faster. Going all in was one of the best decisions we've ever made. That year, I wrote six full length novels and with her behind the helm of the *USS Marketing* we went from just barely scraping by to a thriving business that was booming enough to support not just us, but other authors as well.

Before long, Shadow Alley, my personal joke (I'd come up with the name while trudging through a dark alley in the heart of

Bangkok) was making dreams come true. Five years ago, I never would've believed any of this was possible, and now I can't even envision what my life would look like without this business. At the time of writing this, we've seen another two of our authors go full time, we've sold hundreds of thousands of books, and my wonky stories have taken me all over the globe and earned us more than a million dollars.

Which brings me to my sixth and final point: *It's impossible if you refuse to take the first step.*

There are no guarantees in the business, and there is no surefire way to succeed. None.

You can write the perfect book, sell it to one of the big five publishers, and it can still belly flop like a kid jumping into the pool for the first time. You can also write an amazing story, turn it into a top-notch, professional product, launch it yourself with a great business plan… and still lose every penny. This is a business. Sometimes businesses fail. And you *might* fail if you try, but you will *absolutely* fail if you don't. Moreover, just because you fail once, doesn't mean you can't try again. You can always, always, *always* take another step. I firmly believe that success in publishing is just like success in anything else: it goes to the one who is willing to work hard, learn from past mistakes, and persist long enough to win.

Before you go, remember my third piece of advice: *most people – especially people on the internet – are full of crap and have no idea what they're talking about.* My advice here, like all advice, is wildly subjective, so take it all with a *generous* heaping of salt and if you find none it helpful, disregard and keep on trucking because no one has all the answers and there's no single right way to get to the top of the summit. Good luck and good writing, ink slingers!

Lesons learned:
- ✓ Being clueless doesn't mean you're hopeless
- ✓ Little actions daily, can create big changes when done over time.
- ✓ Most people – especially people on the internet – are full of crap and have no idea what they're talking about.
- ✓ There is no one right way up Dream Mountain.

- ✓ If you want this to be a business, you need to treat it like one.
- ✓ It's impossible if you refuse to take the first step.

*

James A. Hunter is a former Marine, an active member of SFWA, and the best-selling author of the Yancy Lazarus Series, Rogue Dungeon, *and the LitRPG Epic* Viridian Gate Online. *He currently lives in Lexington, Kentucky with his wife and two children, and when not writing or spending time with family, he occasionally finds time to sleep and eat. You can find out more about him, his books, and Shadow Alley Press at www.ShadowAlleyPress.com*

Making My Space
on the Bookshelf

Jana S. Brown

I heard the padding of little feet on stone flooring a moment before the door to my bedroom opened. A small figure shuffled around the bed coming to stand next to me. I squinted to make out the numbers on the clock. 5:05 a.m.

"Mom! I need you."

Her whisper wasn't nearly as quiet as I wished it was, but I'd moved, so I couldn't pretend I didn't hear her.

"What's the matter?"

"I had a nightmare."

I scooted over, making space in the bed for her to climb into. "Go ahead and tell me about it."

Forty minutes later I'd returned my adorable little monster to her bed, told her three stories, and sung two songs. Her soft breathing followed me back to bed where the alarm clock had already started to brighten, *stupid sunrise clock*. I only had about fifteen minutes before the alarm my husband dubbed 'the psycho piano player' would kick off the morning.

Sleep was impossible, but the warm bed called and I slid back in, curling up with my husband and plotting out the chapters I was hoping to get written today. If I could get another 3000 words in it would be excellent, progress. That shouldn't be so hard right?

*

He pulled on her hand and when she stepped closer his arm encircled her waist. Then he was kissing her. This was no chaste kiss on the cheek or teasing peck. This kiss was demanding and devouring. His free hand tangled in her hair as though she might run away if he didn't hold her fast.

"MOM!"

The scream jerked me out of my writing flow and out of my chair. It was the child's cry of pain. I raced through the house to where my daughter was – or at least had been – happily coloring. She still sat there, her big brown eyes tracking my arrival. She held up her finger.

"I pinched my finger."

I stared at her and the tiny pink mark on her fingertip. "Sweetie, you know you're not supposed to yell like that unless there's blood or a fire, right?"

"Yes, but I pinched my finger, and I needed you."

I sighed and sat on the carpet, letting her curl up on my lap. There was a lot more of her to curl these days as the once 19 inch baby now measured at almost 47 inches. She demanded a kiss on her wounded finger and chattered at me until it felt better. I only heard half of her chatter, the rest of my mind still in my book. Just a few hundred more words... I just wanted a few hundred more words.

*

I needed to make a decision about the werewolf council. Given how big the United States was I had to break it down into reasonable territories. I went searching Google for a blank map of the U.S. and grabbed a package of colored pencils. Should it be divided by geography or population?

"Mom?"

I glanced up, meeting the gaze of brown eyes just like mine. "What?"

"That's a really pretty picture you're coloring."

"Thanks."

"Mom?"

"What?"

"I'm hungry. Will you make me a cheese sandwich?"

"We'll have one of those at lunch time, sweetie."

"But it is lunch time."

I shook my head. "Not yet." It couldn't be? Had the time passed so fast? "What time does the clock say?"

She scampered across the room to where she could see the digital clock on the oven. "One. Two. One. One."

12:11.

It was lunch time.

"Okay. Cheese sandwich it is. Go get a *Capri Sun*."

I brought my map with me, assembling lunch with one hand and drawing lines through the states as the cheese on her sandwich melted.

*

I shifted around to get more comfortable, wishing, once again, that I had a dedicated office space, but that hadn't happened yet. I reread the last paragraph, tapping my fingers against the keys without actually typing anything.

"Mom?"

I sighed. Here we went again. "Yes, duckling?"

"I have an idea."

"What's your idea?"

"You've been working on your 'puter for a long time. Maybe we can play the ground is lava now."

I glanced at my word count. 1500. It was half of what I really wanted, but it was progress.

My child smiled and made her patented *'please face'* at me, puckering her lips and squishing up her eyes.

There would be time for more words later. She would be six only once. I hit *save* and pushed the computer away. "The ground is lava! 5-4-3-2-1."

*

My publishing journey started early, around the same age as the little girl on my couch. When you ask that little girl what she wants to be when she grows up her answers vary based on the day, her mood, and what show she last saw on YouTube or television that has her thinking. This week she's had goals to be a princess, a ballerina, an astronaut, and a volunteer at the Humane Society. I'm sure I went through some of these options, but most often – as reported by my mother – from the time I picked up my first pencil, I wanted to grow up to be an author and a mommy. Eventually, I managed both, but neither was as easy as 6-year-old me thought it would be. It took me a long time to find my family and longer to make my space on the bookshelf.

My first ventures into getting published started with reading everything I could get my hands on, and writing any chance I found a paper and pen. Summer days were spent biking with my siblings to the Public Library where I worked my way through the children's section and had to get my mother to check out books for me from the adult section. I liked reading a variety of material, but early on I knew speculative fiction with a hint of romance was my jam. Tolkein, Eddings, McCaffery, Fisher, Asimov, Norton, Weis and Hickman were only a few of the names that filled my shelves side-by-side with fairytale collections and the best of Nancy Drew. I read them all and spent hours retelling them to my siblings, learning the patterns of stories and language. Everywhere I went a book, a pen, and a notebook came along, and I scrawled out imperfect short stories and poetry while trying to figure out the tricks of long form.

I taught myself to touch type on an old typewriter with the keys blacked out and went through far too much white out trying to make every story perfect. Then in the late 80's my parents purchased our first family computer complete with a word processing program, and I fought for time to type between my siblings' games of *Tetris* and some racing game I can't remember the title of. At the age of fourteen, encouraged by positive feedback from teachers and parents, I typed 'The End' on my first full length novel.

It was a beautiful thing, my novel. It was 230 pages of inserting my friends into a Tolkienish fantasy quest complete with songs, and romance, and adventure. It was highly derivative and lacked polish – things I didn't know at the time – but it was mine. It took nearly every bit of babysitting money I had to get it printed on something better quality than our dot matrix printer and to package it up and post it off to New York. There, at the offices of Tor Publishing, I was fated to be the next teenage phenomenon.

I waited for my SASE to return, or for a phone call, for some hint of how well I'd done. It took nearly three months, during which I worked on book two because, naturally, this was going to be a trilogy, but the SASE came back. Enclosed was my first real rejection.

Thank you for sending The DragonEyes for our consideration, but we are unable to publish it at this time.

The words were a punch to the gut. I'd been so sure I was ready. So confident.

Congratulations on finishing your book. I encourage you to keep reading and keep writing. Keep working on your craft, and I'm sure one day you'll be published.

This part wasn't so bad. In fact this part wasn't bad at all. I just had to try harder. I could do that. I had more stories to tell. I was going to be on those bookshelves. I just knew it.

(It would be years before I'd realize how rare it was to get a personalized response and encouragement. I keep that rejection letter close to hand so I can reread it every time I need a pick me up.)

So I kept at it. All through high school and into college I wrote and wrote. I filled notebooks and 3.5 inch floppy disks with ideas and stories both finished and half-baked. I wrote for the school year book and entered pieces into every local contest I found. In college I studied linguistics, and editing, and a creative writing class focused on writing science fiction and fantasy with the amazing Professor Marion Smith, who understood story and depth in a way I've never seen matched. He was fondly referred to as "Doc" Smith and the *Life the Universe and Everything Symposium* still bears his name. He pushed me to write outside of my comfort zone and not to rest on the encouragement I'd already received, but to get more aggressive.

I did.

And I got more rejections.

None of them as nice as the first one.

But I kept working. During this time I also discovered online email writing groups. Some were critique groups and others were based on collaborative storytelling. I wrote and wrote exploring characters and themes and learning how to work with other authors to weave a story. None of it would ever be publishable, but it felt like every word made me better.

The other college courses that proved themselves massively valuable were my technical writing courses and my editing for publication course. Through my editing work I joined the staff of *The Leading Edge: Magazine of Science Fiction and Fantasy*. It was my first time working on such a publication, and over two years I worked at almost every position. I was selected as the Executive Secretary for the magazine a few months in. I opened the mail, sent out form rejections, filed and sorted entries, read and edited stories and poetry, completed typesetting, took subscriptions, and mailed out the completed magazines. It was the most intensive publication education I've ever received and honed skills I use to this day.

Heading out into the work force after college I found that there weren't a lot of opportunities that called for my fiction writing skills. I was still sending manuscripts into the dark and still getting rejections. Sometimes form letters, and occasionally those very precious personalized rejections. Sometimes only the sound of silence. The skills I had were most marketable were my technical writing abilities, my editorial eye, my organizational bent, and my technological abilities. I couldn't make much money writing fiction, but I could make a decent living creating technical manuals and quality assurance reports.

Over the next few years, I published a lot of technical articles and manuals, and I served as a Senior Editor for a medical transcription company – among others. I was making a mark in newsprint and reviewing games for online sites as the use of the Internet blossomed. I was busy and doing well, even if it wasn't what I'd pictured.

I hadn't left fiction entirely, I still wrote volumes in online RPGs and filled notebooks with my scribbles, but, for a while, it seemed like finding my spot on the fiction bookshelves was a losing battle. I never really stopped working on my creative writing during this time, but I slowed down on turning it in for queries. I was feeling a little bruised from all my brushes with 'this isn't right for our needs at this time' and 'well written, but really didn't work for me,' and I needed a break.

Added to my lack of progress on the dating front, it seemed that both of my childhood goals were falling flat.

So what made the difference?

A persistent story.

The birth of self-publishing.

A supportive man.

Though really those are backward in order, the man came first. In 2006 a friend announced that he was getting divorced. I was recently out of a bad relationship myself and so we banded together to denounce the evils of romance and relationships, thus beginning the year of 'no, we're not dating we just talk a lot and hang out.'

I can't say that my muse was suddenly inspired or that I wrote and published a million books that year, but something did change. I had someone who I talked to every day and who loved books and reading as much as I did. He asked what I was working on, and I sent him snatches and scenes to read. Within a few months I had a fan club – it was a fan club of one, but it reminded me of what I wanted, of what I had always wanted. I had stories in my blood, and they needed to get out there into the world.

As hanging out turned into dating, and eventually marriage, the first version of what would be *Fallen Stone*, my first urban fantasy, was born. The first chapter won several contests and Tor books requested the first three chapters, and then the whole manuscript. This was the moment... it was all going to...

Get rejected again.

This time with a six month wait and the stunning sound of silence.

At the same time we were struggling with our new little family as we figured out how to be husband and wife to each other and father and step-mother to his young sons. We were both working full time and taking on the boys as much as we could. Time was tight. We wanted another child, but it wasn't happening, and I started infertility treatments which made me crazy(er).

I was hard to block out a chunk of time to work, so I took to writing in the corners and around the edges of my life. I found thirty minutes here, and forty minutes there. I wrote during lunch breaks and family parties. I finished a novel with a co-author and sent it out for queries.

We got a rewrite and resubmit request.

This was the moment.

It was all going to…

Fall to pieces. My co-author was getting married and getting her degree, and she was so busy she didn't know her left hand from her right (not that this was her fault, the timing was sucktastic) and the changes we needed to make had to be done together. We missed the deadline to turn the manuscript back and the opportunity fell to dust.

My husband helped me scrape my bruised ego up off the ground. He was again my fan club of one and assured me my writing was amazing and was going to go somewhere. He really loved the idea for *Fallen Stone* but he'd support any story I wrote. I decided to keep working.

One lazy Sunday afternoon I flopped on the floor and scribbled out the outline for a novel. From beginning to end it took me about an hour and it felt really solid, but it was a science fiction, western, romance and I'd never written a book that was primarily romance. I sent the outline to a good friend who read a lot of romance. He loved it and told me to write it now.

Desert Rains felt like it wrote itself. It flowed out in about six months – around full time work and parenting. My husband held down the fort, and I would retreat to my basement writing desk and make words until my fingers were too cold. During the last part of that six months, after we'd given up on fertility treatments, I became pregnant with our daughter.

I sent the book out for consideration.

I had a baby.

An editor who I was friendly with from online chats got a hold of the manuscript.

She told me it was good. She told me it was publishable.

Then she told me she couldn't take it because there was no slot for a science fiction western romance.

I'm fairly certain that was the point when my brain exploded. It was so frustrating to be told I was good enough, but not marketable enough.

However, things were changing in publishing and there were other options. A good friend had recently delved deep into the realm of self-publishing. She had the ability to publish the types of stories she wanted at the pace she wanted, and was seeing success. I talked to my supportive husband, and he agreed there was no reason to wait anymore for traditional publishing to tell me I was good enough. We'd make the space on the bookshelf for me ourselves.

My friend walked me through all the steps for self-publishing (the writing community is really a wonderful place filled with wonderful people). I got my book edited, hired my brother to make me a cover, and launched my first novel, *Desert Rains*, in October 2015.

Since that time I've put together two cookbooks, three novels (*Desert Rains*, *Fallen Stone* and *Said in Stone*), and been featured in two anthologies. I work as a freelance editor to help others reach their dreams, and I keep my fingers in the technical writing pie. My daughter is young so I still write in the corners. I scribble on napkins at McDonalds, and take notebooks with me to the park.

I don't publish as fast as some of the writers I know because sometimes the floor is lava, and it's important to spend time with my daughter while she's still young enough to want to spend time with me, but the stories in my blood are alive and my direction is secure. That list of published titles is only going to grow!

So what did I learn through all of this?

1: Never give up, never surrender.

Even at my lowest, I never stopped writing. I love telling stories, and I never let the rejections kill that love. If you have stories to be told, never stop telling them – even if you keep them to yourself for a while.

2: Big or small, find your tribe.

You need to find those people who are your support group, whether inside of your family or out of it. Earlier on I referred to my husband as being my fan club of one, but it was a very important fan club at an important point in my career. He doesn't read romance, but he was the first person to buy my science fiction western romance novel. He always reminds me that he thinks I'm a fantastic writer and everyone needs someone like that in their corner.

My grandmother buys everything I write. She sometimes raises her eyebrows over the language my characters use, (Sorry, Grandma!) but all of my books are on her shelves. She's so proud of her granddaughter the writer.

I also have friends in the writing community who give me support and allow me to support them in return. Knowing you aren't alone on the journey of publishing is both an amazing lift and a great kick in the pants to keep you going. My writing partner and her husband – who we like to call the Plot Whisperer – keep up the encouragement while ruthlessly pointing out where I've gone wrong and pushing me to do it right. My writing is better for their input.

3: Sometimes the ground is lava.

I use this to refer to the need to take care of my family as well as my writing, but it can apply to all kinds of things in your real life. Take care of yourself, physically, mentally, spiritually, and emotionally. Stress can kill a writing career, so you've got to know when it's time to push the computer away and take a trip, or spend time with friends and family, or just stretch out in the sunshine and pet a puppy.

Work-life balance can be hard when you're a writer because you live at your work. You have to find a schedule that works for you to be able to give what's needed to both.

4: Don't be afraid to branch out.

I learned so much in my years of technical writing. All of that writing taught me to be a better writer as well as paying the bills and building my writing resume. It was writing something I'd never done before that finally pushed me into self-publishing and solidified my brand as the author who "writes the weird and the wonderful... with smoochies."

5: There are no wasted words.

If I were to count up all the words I've written since I was that six-year-old child they would number around two to three million, give or take. Of those millions I've probably published about one million or so between my technical work, short stories, and my novels.

Those other words are not wasted words.

Every piece I wrote was a chance to work on my craft, to experiment with where stories could go and with what I wanted to be as a writer. Every story was an opportunity and many of those ideas I'll revisit as I continue to grow my booklist. I am better for the words that were bad, and better still for the ones that were good.

*

"Mom! I'm home from my play date."

I pushed myself away from the computer and gave my little girl a hug. "Did you have a good time?"

"Yes! We went to the park and ate blue popsicles."

Her blue lips were hard to miss.

"I'm glad. Should we go make dinner?"

"Yes! Hot dogs, please! Are you finished on the 'puter?"

"For today."

Lesons learned:
- ✓ Never give up, never surrender.
- ✓ Big or small, find your tribe.
- ✓ Don't be afraid to branch out.
- ✓ There are no wasted words.
- ✓ Sometimes the ground is lava.

*

When Jana S. Brown was eight, she wanted to be an author and a mother. Now she's both, complete with fuzzy sidekicks, and writes the weird and the wonderful with smoochies. Her published fiction works include Desert Rains, Fallen Stone, *and* Said in Stone *and short stories in the anthologies* Love Undefined, Wings of Change, *and* Love Among the Thorns.

Selling My First Non-fiction Book and My First Novel

Carolyn Rae Williamson

I wanted to learn to write a book about my experiences working in a federal prison, so I joined the DFW (Dallas-Fort Worth) Writer's Workshop. The group meets weekly to hear writers read their work and offer helpful suggestions.

However, while learning how to write, I got sidetracked by a great idea at a writer's conference I attended with two diabetic friends. My husband had recently been diagnosed with heart problems. Using the knowledge I gained as a home economics major in college, I knew the dietary requirements for diabetes and heart problems were similar: less fat, less sugar, less salt, and less calories, so I knew how to develop suitable recipes for people who cooked for heart patients, diabetics, or dieters. I suggested to my friends that we collaborate on a cookbook and stopped work on the prison book.

Developing the Cookbook

My friends, Pepper Durcholz and Alberta Gentry, (now deceased) were excited about writing a cookbook with me, so we hauled out our favorite family recipes. I figured out how to cut fat, sugar, and salt. However, it wasn't so easy. Sometimes after making the altered recipes, we found the foods didn't taste good. We tried again, sometimes as many as five times for a single dish, before coming up with good results. We twisted arms of willing guinea pigs, our friends, relatives, and members of writer's groups to taste our foods. They never knew what to expect from us. One night, Pepper made cookies for her daughter and boyfriend to snack on when they came home. She used all the sugar and butter from the original recipe, but the next morning, the cookies were untouched. When asked, her daughter said, "I thought they were the diet version, so we didn't eat them."

Once the recipes passed the taste-test, we had to figure out the nutrient content. This was prior to the passage of nutrient labeling requirements, which meant we had to look up the amounts for each ingredient in the *Nutrient Value of Foods,* published by the United States Department of Agriculture. It took lots of arithmetic to get the amounts for each serving.

Finally, after three years, we were ready to produce a cookbook. I compiled everything into one digital file and prepared to sell it to a publisher. A fellow writer, who'd been on many diets, had once asked, "Is there life after lettuce?" providing the inspiration for our title, *There IS Life After Lettuce.*

Pitching the Cookbook

I used Jeff Herman's excellent book, *How to Write a Book Proposal*, as a guide and prepared a book proposal, complete with a list of types of people who might buy the book, a table of contents, sample chapters, and sample recipes with calories and nutrients listed. I also entered the book into two writer's contests, and it won first and second place with checks for $100 and $50.

I sent the proposals to editors at several publishing houses, but none seemed interested. I hadn't expected it would take three years to sell our cookbook. Then the DFW Writer's Workshop invited Ed Eakin, an editor from an Austin, Texas, publisher, to speak. I volunteered to take him to the airport and took advantage of the opportunity to tell him about *There IS Life After Lettuce.* He sounded interested, but said they had already contracted for as many books as they could handle that year, but that I could try again in a year.

We waited a year, sent him the proposal, and waited with fingers crossed. But when he finally responded, it was with a rejection letter saying he didn't know how to market such a book. I got busy and wrote up a marketing plan, listing bookstores where we could arrange signings and possible newspaper columns that might feature the book. Then Pepper and I made an appointment to meet with him, and drove three hours to Eakin Press in Austin. At last, after trying to sell it for three years, the editor looked at our proposed marketing plan and agreed to publish the book.

Outside, we walked to Pepper's van with springs in our steps. We raised our fists in the air, and shouted, "All right!" A sprinkler came on and sprayed us, but we didn't care.

Signing a Contract Should be Easy, Shouldn't It?

All three of us rode to Austin to sign the contract. By now, I'd talked to other successful writers and knew what to ask for. I outlined all our requests. Mr. Eakin said he wasn't going to pay royalties on the cover price, only the wholesale one. He wouldn't include pictures of food. After hearing our other requests, the editor shook his head and said, "You three need to go home and think this over."

Shocked and disappointed, I swallowed a gasp. Maybe if I pushed for things he might agree on, we could still save the sale. About that time, my diabetic co-author, Pepper, asked me if I had any candy. She had been so nervous that her blood sugar was way down. I found a Lifesaver in my purse for her, and soon she was better.

Pushing down my anxiety and trying to show a brave front, I asked the editor what he *would* agree to. The editor finally agreed to provide ten copies for each of us, instead of ten total, and to give us our rights back six months after requesting them. He allowed us to keep our rights to sell pot holders and aprons in connection with our books, although we hadn't planned to do that.

He assigned us an editor and paid someone in Dallas, near my house, to design our cover, so I could meet him and explain what we wanted. A writer friend, Neil Ross, (now deceased) who owned an advertising agency, advised me what to request for the front cover, a layout of foods to show readers there was a lot of food they could eat, despite their dietary restrictions.

While waiting for publication, we received edits from Mr. Eakin. Among the revisions he'd asked for, he suggested we change the title because bookstore employees wouldn't know where to stock it. We called several bookstores and were assured they could figure out *There IS Life After Lettuce* was a cookbook. After reporting back to Mr. Eakin, he agreed to keep the title.

Publication at Last!

When copies of the book arrived at my house, I was so excited. Even though my articles had been printed in newspapers and magazines, I was now an author of a published book. Because my co-authors and I all lived in different towns, we each went out to dinner with our husbands to celebrate.

A local, friendly bookstore invited us to do a book signing. Pepper, Alberta, and I cooked up samples from our cookbook, invited the DFW Writer's Workshop, and served them at the store. We sold forty copies that day, and many more at different bookstores in the Dallas-Fort Worth area in the months following. Shy Alberta got very good at walking around and offering sample cookies we'd made for the different signings, but some people still only approached our table to ask where the restroom was.

Whenever I visited the nearby Half-Price used bookstore, I looked for our cookbook. I hated to think that anyone would want to get rid of the book we'd worked so hard on. One day I was disappointed to see not one, but *two* copies there. Days later, I decided I should buy them and try to sell them to someone else, so I went back, but they were gone.

What I Wished I'd Known Earlier

While thrilled to autograph copies at one bookstore, I noticed they'd arranged the book way down in the W's (for Williamson), even though we'd listed Pepper Durcholz as the first author. I looked at all the other cookbooks, amazed at how many there were. If I'd realized the amount of the competition, we might not have tried to finish it, but I'm glad we did.

I hadn't realized that small publishers often pay royalties on the *wholesale* price instead of the *retail* price, or that we'd get no royalties on copies we bought to sell on our own since we bought them at a discount. In order to avoid that, we arranged for a local distributor to buy copies for us and paid them for the books.

I also didn't realize that just having our book listed in a catalogue sent to stores all over the U.S. wouldn't get our books into all those stores. It was only when Mr. Eakin visited Barnes and Noble distributors in certain states and got them to agree to purchase a certain number of books in Oklahoma, Texas, Louisiana, and Tennessee, that the books were put on the shelves in those states, but probably not in others.

Another unwelcome surprise included finding typos, such as *1 ½ cup of __* but which didn't name the ingredient, in the printed books, even though we'd each checked the galley proofs. We had to print up slips of paper listing the typos to include with each book we signed at book signings.

One bookstore requested we prepare several items to cook at the store. We had so much stuff to carry in, that Pepper claimed we were becoming pack animals, but we sold twenty-five copies that day. However, at most stores, we'd only sell around six copies. I also learned I needed to arrange a book signing to get book stores to order more books after they ran out.

One bookstore didn't get copies in time, so we had to bring our own. Later I had to drive to the other side of Dallas to pick up the twenty-five copies they returned to us.

We sold all the copies that were printed, so we can be proud of that. Since there is only one similar book listed on Amazon, Pepper and I are busy getting a sequel ready, which we plan to call *More Than Lettuce*. However, now agents and editors want authors to have a *platform*, with many readers on Facebook, that they be a famous personality, or even have a television show before they'll consider publishing their cookbook. I'm still waiting to hear from one agent who has our proposal.

Another agent I approached, rejected our proposal, but suggested ten cookbook agents who might do better at selling it, so I will query them. Hopefully, Pepper and I will find a publisher for *More Than Lettuce*.

Selling my First Novel

Although I'd been writing and submitting romance novels—they interested me more than the prison one—it wasn't until several years later after I submitted my thirteenth manuscript to Noble Romance, that I landed a sale. Wow. I'd sold my first novel! I was excited and could hardly wait until it got published.

During the next eight months, Noble Romance edited my manuscript and sent me a copy of a really nice cover. The Dallas Area Romance Authors presented me with a white rose, their customary award for a first sale. I ordered 300 pens imprinted with my name, the book's title, and Noble Romance, but waited for publication to begin handing them out as advertising.

When I e-mailed Noble Romance, asking for a publication date, I received a letter saying they had decided to stop publishing novels.

I was so disappointed. But I didn't give up. After Noble Romance cancelled my contract, I submitted the manuscript to other publishers, but it kept getting rejected. Then a friend who had books published by MuseItUp suggested I try them.

MuseItUp accepted the book and edited it in seven months. They even created a cover similar to the one I'd liked before. Afraid to believe it would really happen, I crossed my fingers until it actually appeared on Amazon as available for preorder. It was finally published on September 26, 2014. Now I could really celebrate! My local romance writers' group, North Texas RWA, gave me a 5 X 7 glass-enclosed copy of my cover, which I keep on a shelf above my desk.

What I Wished I had Known Sooner

Some small publishers help a little with promotion, but most don't. My second novel, published by Wild Rose Press, has received a little publisher help, but MuseItUp Publishing did not do anything other than make it available for pre-order. However, MuseItUp did keep the print copy priced at under ten dollars, while Wild Rose Press has posted the price as $16.99, so it can't compete with most printed copies of romance books, which are priced at $7.99.

Also, both small publishers had their print copies available only on a print-on-demand basis, so people have to ask for them by name at a brick-and-mortar store instead of find them on the shelves. I have to set up a book signing in order to get my books into a bookstore.

Self-Publishing Costs

I'm now a hybrid author, with books for sale from publishers and self-published books available through Amazon. When I self-published my Witness Protection Series, I paid for editing and cover design, and discovered I also needed to pay for formatting for the Kindle and the Nook. I also learned that printed copies from Amazon's Create Space (now Kindle Direct Publishing), are not accepted by Barnes and Noble, but Ingram Spark prints books are (note that there is a set-up fee for publishing through Ingram Spark).

Promoting on the Internet

From a course given by the Romance Writers of America (RWA), I learned to set up my website. I quickly discovered that if I checked to see if a domain name was available, if I didn't register the name right away, it would later be offered at a price over and above the registration price. I also found that for an extra fee, I can keep my personal contact information private. I chose WordPress for my hosting at a nominal cost, and I've even posted an audio chapter from one of my books that my neighbor, a former broadcaster, narrated for me.

Promoting on Facebook

I set up a profile Facebook page under my legal name, Carolyn Rae Williamson, as required, and also set up a "Carolyn Rae Author" Facebook page, but I soon learned that Facebook doesn't send what I write on either page to all the friends I have accumulated. Facebook wants me to spend money on advertising, but their cheapest option, Boost Your Post, only goes to people living in and around the area where I live, although I can choose an age range for recipients.

Now, as a hybrid author of ten books, I plan to continue submitting some of my books to publishers and self-publishing others.

In the meantime, I have revised and republished *Pretend Princess*, now available on Amazon, as the first book in a trilogy with my Kindle World books, *Royal Wedding Scoop* and *Holiday with a Royal* which I now have the rights to. The characters have been transplanted from the world of the Royals of Monterra to the Cordillera Royals, in Cordillera, a small fictional kingdom between France and Spain. All the heroines will be U.S. women who manage to win the hearts of wonderful princes. I'm also working on a fourth book with a heroine who has a secret background.

Lesons learned:
- ✓ It takes really wanting to achieve publication
- ✓ It takes perseverance
- ✓ It takes more work than I expected.

*

Carolyn Rae Williamson follows her passion, writing romantic suspense where bullets are flying, people are dying, and lovers are resisting attraction until they can escape the danger following them.

She is the author of Romancing the Gold *and* Romancing the Doctor, Searching for Love, Pretend Princess, Royal Wedding Scoop, *and the* Witness Protection Series *trilogy.*

She is also one of the co-authors of There IS Life After Lettuce, *a cookbook for heart patients and diabetics. Her profile and travel articles have appeared in* The Dallas Morning News, *the* Fort Worth Star Telegram, *and* Romance Writer's Report.

We Are All Storytellers
Lauryn Christopher

Despite the fact that I couldn't properly diagram a sentence if my life depended on it, my high-school English teacher told me I had a way with words, and suggested that if I didn't have other career plans, I might want to look into something like journalism or advertising, where I could capitalize on that skillset.

It felt like fortune-cookie advice at the time, but I respected the teacher and his opinions, so I looked. To be perfectly honest, I also looked at accounting and teaching and professional horse-training and technical theater and architecture and law and psychology – which is to say that I took a long, convoluted stroll through the halls of higher education.

Sadly, the professional horse-training program was so far out of the budget that I never got beyond looking – longingly – at the brochures (this might be an entirely different essay had price not been a factor!). But while I amassed more than my share of credits (and a couple of degrees) in some of those other areas of study, none had thoroughly captured my interest to the extent of being something I thought I wanted to do with the rest of my life.

Oddly enough, all that wandering only took me into the English department twice.

The first time was for a class on writing research papers that I needed to fill a degree requirement. As a lark, I also happened to be playing around with my first attempt at writing a novel at the time (it was what all the bookish girls in the dorm were doing that semester), so instead of choosing from the list of "approved" (aka, standard, boring, and done-to-death) topics, my research topics went a little off-list.

I wrote a paper on medieval castles and the culture/economics of the surrounding cities because I was setting my book in that period. I wrote a paper on vampire legends and lore so I could better depict my book's dark and brooding hero. And – this was a good one – I even wrote a paper on "time travel as depicted in film and literature," because time travel was a central theme of the book.

The essays got high marks, probably as much for their novelty as for the actual writing. And learning to distill what I'd researched into the papers taught me a lot about research for fiction writing. Only a fraction of what I'd learned went into those papers; now, only a fraction of what I research about any given topic ever makes it into a story – just enough to make it feel "real," without going overboard into exhaustive info-dumps and monologues by know-it-all characters.

My writing alternated between essays for my class and working on the book, but after two months, eight chapters, and about twenty-seven thousand words, the book stalled and was eventually relegated to the "maybe I'll resurrect it one day" files. I'd gotten far enough into it to realize that while I routinely devoured entire libraries' worth of novels, and knew a lot about storytelling from the *outside*, I didn't actually know a thing about *writing* fiction.

But I'd also gotten far enough into the book to have been bitten by the writing bug. If I could figure out how to write a novel without having to diagram a sentence or memorize volumes of grammar books, I wanted to give it a go.

During the very last semester of college, I signed up for the second English class of my career. At the time, I didn't know if the instructor had written or published anything – something I generally look for now, when considering a class or workshop offering – but he knew how to teach story structure, which made the class exactly what I was looking for. He also knew how to offer criticism and advice to new writers in a way that helped them strengthen their own stories rather than turn their work into something he might have created out of the same basic idea.

While none of the stories I wrote during that class were what one would consider enduring works of literature – none of them topped 1800 words – I learned a great deal from the class. I discovered the character-setting-conflict structure at the heart of a story. I learned about basic elements of plot and story arc.

And I learned that if I wanted to tell the stories buzzing around my head, I had *so much more* to learn.

*

Flash forward a few years. I'd met a bunch of other writers, joined a critique group, attended writing conferences. I'd sat in classes taught by well-respected authors, and taken copious notes. I didn't write every day (I had a day job to work around and toddlers underfoot at home), but I wrote regularly, practicing what I was learning. And though I had little expectation of actually *selling* anything at this point, I had started submitting stories to magazines on a fairly consistent basis.

I figured, why not? The worst they could do was say no, and hey, it was possible someone might actually buy one. A miracle could happen. After all, my writing was getting a little better with every new story I wrote, and besides, what was the point of writing if I kept all my stories hidden away in my files?

One of the benefits of being part of a writers' group was that I'd developed a thick skin when it came to feedback. It came as no surprise that my stories wouldn't appeal to everyone, but learning how to interpret their feedback and how – or more importantly, *when* – to incorporate their suggestions into my work was an important lesson. Because here's the thing: when one person has a problem with something in your story, it could be a problem, or it could just be how the story hit them in the moment.

But stories are a lot like intricately designed Rube Goldberg inventions (though the better ones are far less over-engineered!), and the gun on the mantelpiece in chapter one and man hiding in the shadows in chapter two combine to set off a chain reaction of expectations for the reader. I learned that when multiple readers had problems at/near the same point in a story, it was worth taking a more critical look at not just the item they'd all called out, but at the other things leading up to it, to see where information may have been presented in the wrong order or the chain of events had gone awry.

I didn't feel ready yet to dive back into writing a novel, so I kept practicing my skills on short stories. And as time passed, I wrote a lot of stories, submitted them everywhere, and collected lots of rejections. And that was another important thing I learned from being around other writers – I wasn't the only one getting rejection letters! Of course I already knew that *logically*, but it helped to take away some of the sting when other people you knew and whose stories you'd thought were pretty good, were also getting turned away.

We'd all heard, from conference speakers, about the "food chain" of rejection letters. If you haven't yet heard of it, let me explain. Editors are very busy, and receive far too many submissions to respond personally to every one (or even many) of them. So they'll often use form letters, just to save time. However, there's sort of a hierarchy to the rejection letters they send out that goes something like this:

- *"Thanks for submitting, it didn't work for us"* = Means exactly what it says. It doesn't mean your story sucks.
- *"Thanks for submitting, we're not taking this one but look forward to seeing your next"* = Again, means what it says, but also means that the editor saw something in your work that made it stand out to them.
- *The above form letter, with a line or two added from the first reader/editor* = Means they liked your work, and while they can't take it for this project, they want to be encouraging.
- *An entirely personal note* from the editor that talks about specific things in your story, recommends you send it to a sister publication, etc. = No promises, but if you hit this editor with the right story, for the right project, at the right time, they're probably going to buy it.

(Note: Every editor has their own set of form letters – and some houses don't even bother to respond to stories they're not taking – so take this list with a grain of salt.)

The more I wrote, the better my stories got – as measured by my gradual movement up the rejection ladder. Now that's not to say that a great story won't ever get a straight form rejection, they will, but the responses tend to move toward the last two types as you get better. It's an editor's way of encouraging you.

*

Life can be inconvenient, and I found myself a single mom with young children. By then I'd ghost-written on a couple of non-fiction projects, was working part-time as a technical writer (all that college education had to add up to something marketable, right?) and had sold a couple of short stories for enough to splurge on a nice dinner out. I'd written a novel that I was trying to sell, and was sketching out the bones for a new novel.

And then I found myself facing the choice of writing for pennies per word (fiction) or dollars per hour (not fiction).

I had children to feed. I chose dollars per hour.

It was years before I did any serious fiction writing again. If I had it to do over, I would have made the same decision, but I would have tried to slip more short fiction into the cracks, just to keep my skills from rusting over, and sent them out, so the editors and readers didn't forget my name. Would have revised and continued to market that early book (which one editor told me was very good but needed specific revisions) instead of putting it in a drawer where it still sits to this day. But that's all hindsight.

At the time, I told a friend – who was also a respected mentor and NYT bestselling author – that I *"...felt like a has-been wanna-be."* I believed my fiction writing career was over before it had really even gotten started.

I remember his response as though it was yesterday. He shook his head and said, "We've all hit bumps and roadblocks, some bigger than others – every writer does. And when life knocks us down, sometimes it takes a while to get back up. But you're a writer, a storyteller – it's part of who you are. So go, do what you need to do now, to take care of your family. And when the time is right, and you come back, the words will still be there."

I held onto that for years, like a lifeline.

And while writing in the corporate world wasn't exercising all of the same muscles as writing fiction, the work did keep my writing muscles from atrophying completely. And I grew in other ways. I developed the confidence in my ability to string words together in a form that people not only liked to read, but were willing to pay for. I learned basic business skills that served me well as a freelancer, and which have since made learning about the business side of publishing (traditional and indie) much easier *(you've got to understand contracts and copyright and royalties and money-management – but that's a whole different essay!)*

And all the while, I kept my eyes open, jotting down notes for future stories.

Because my friend was right. I am a storyteller. I have a writer's brain. In a delightful essay, Neil Gaiman once said, *"...You get ideas all the time. The only difference between writers and other people is we notice when we're doing it..."* I know exactly what he's talking about – and if you're reading this, you do, too.

I walk into a room and think about how it's laid out and where the antagonist would hide the body or which door the heroine would escape through. I overhear a bit of conversation and wrap an entire scene around it. I try to figure out the story that would connect two songs on an album.

I think in story.

I could write all day long every day for the rest of my life and still never write all the story ideas I've already had, much less the ones that will occur to me between now and then. But that's not going to stop me from trying.

It took quite a while for life to settle out to the point where I could start writing again on a regular basis, but I did finally come back to fiction. In the last few years, I've written and published a handful of novels, under this and other names, along with quite a few short stories. I've written stories inspired by the notes I took during the non-writing years, and I've written stories I never would have attempted if not because of a particular challenge or open anthology call. I've learned – *mostly*, because it's an ongoing process – to get out of my own way and just let the story tell itself.

I never did finish that novel I started in college – I don't know if I ever will. And my degrees didn't take me to either journalism or marketing (specifically), even though I've written peripherally in both fields. But my high-school English teacher was right when he nudged me in the direction of a career in writing – and I told him so when I went back to the school and gave him an autographed copy of the anthology containing my first published short story.

I have to tell you, the smile that lit up his face was worth all the wandering down the convoluted paths it took to find my way back to that classroom.

Lessons learned:
- ✓ Consume "story" in any form – read short stories and novels and graphic novels. If you don't have a lot of time to read, listen to audiobooks. Study movies and television. Let story structure and character development soak into your subconscious.
- ✓ Write to your strengths – find themes, topics, styles, forms you enjoy.
- ✓ Write out of your comfort zone – keep from falling into a rut by trying something new on a regular basis.
- ✓ Always be learning – keeping your eyes and ears and mind open lets you absorb new ideas and concepts and material you can incorporate into your work.
- ✓ Always be learning more about the craft – seek out teachers and mentors who are farther along the road and incorporate what works for you into your process.
- ✓ Don't give up – when life throws roadblocks in your path (and it will), do what you need to do to deal with the situation. Take care of your family and yourself. The words will still be there when you come back.

*

As a mystery reader, Lauryn Christopher likes figuring out "whodunit" as much as anyone – but as a mystery writer with a background in psychology, she's much more likely to write from the culprit's point of view, exploring the hidden secrets driving their choices. You can see this in the crime fiction and cozy capers she contributes to various anthologies, as well as in her "Hit Lady for Hire" novels. Read Lauryn's musings on storytelling, find links to more of her work, and sign up for her occasional newsletter on her website: www.laurynchristopher.com

How to Cut 77 Years Off Your Road to Success (aka: Don't Do This!)

Tracy Cooper-Posey

Who am I to tell you what not to do?

Fair question.

I've been writing so long, that when I first set out to be published, the *only* choice was traditional publishing. I've been through every iteration of writing and publishing genre fiction known to man and seen it from the inside, where the levers and pulleys creak and grind.

I'm not a name bestseller. I've never appeared on the *New York Times* list, or the *USA Today* Bestseller list. I *have* hit the Amazon #1 spot (yes, in the entire store), for a whole single day, back when there were not seven million titles on Amazon, and big promo pushes could spike your book higher and higher as readers took notice.

You likely had not heard my name before reaching this essay in the collection.

That's fine, though, because I am a solid indie mid-list author who has made her living from writing genre fiction for several years. There are several thousand romance readers who *adore* my books and snap up anything I write, as soon as I release it. I'm at the pleasurable place where I can spend most of my day writing fiction, and get paid enough to cover my living expenses.

I'm still working toward the next tiers of success, because this is an open-ended game.

I've been writing and publishing for decades. That gives me the benefit of hindsight gained through experience. I've learned one or two things along the way, that, had I known about them *much* earlier, would have considerably shortened my path to my first definition of success: Quitting the day job to write fiction full time.

Rather than give you iron-clad rules, though, I want to point out errors in *approach*. Rules won't help you, because in five minutes' time, they'll be irrelevant. The genre fiction world changes *that* fast.

You're better off building a framework for your writing business against which you can test any new idea or strategy, or even the hottest, greatest breakthrough in publishing (available for the next twelve hours for a measly $300 a month), and measure if the idea will work for you.

That alone will save you oodles of time... but I'll get to that, below.

Don't Get Into This Business Unless You Really Love Reading and Books

I was tempted to phrase this as: *Don't get into the business unless you love writing.* Only, how can you know if you love writing until you actually, you know, write?

However, a love of *reading books* in particular is a good benchmark that you might like writing.

Less relevant, but still a fairly good marker, is if you love story-telling of any sort: If you watch movies and TV series all the time; if you're obsessed about Manga; if you love long role-playing video games.

My son, for example, is deeply involved in playing Dungeons & Dragons. He has studied carefully and turned himself into one of the most sought-after Dungeon Masters in the city. Although he vociferously denies it, what he's doing is telling stories. One day I suspect he might turn to telling a less fluid type of story typically found in novels.

These are all hints that you might like telling stories, but you must also develop a love of the writing process, the act of getting words onto paper (or pixels onto a screen). This is the *only* intrinsic reward in this business and you will go a long, long time (twenty years, in my case) with no other rewards in sight. Something must sustain you through the endless hard times and challenges. Loving what you do is therefore essential and will drive you onward.

In the early years of indie publishing, scammers and entrepreneur types zeroed in on the industry as a quick way to earn their next fortune. For a few years, it was impossible to avoid tripping over thirty page "books" of regurgitated factoids, with slick marketing and packaging, that made their "author" thousands of dollars. These days, those shoddy products are harder to find, because the fly-by-night operators figured the profit margins in publishing are just not worth the hassle.

(On the other hand, the con artists developed a dozen other ways to rig the system in their favour, which are only indirectly related to writing novels.)

If you're in the business because you love the act of writing, then you'll find a way to make it work.

My bookkeeper has often suggested, with a straight face, that I look for an alternative revenue stream, because this one is not very profitable, and I should diversify.

...and do what? That's the blank I come up with. Anything else wouldn't be writing.

So I keep writing.

Yes, you might hit the best-seller lists, make millions and cover yourself in glory. In fact, there are more mega-successful indie authors than there ever were traditionally published authors. That mega success is *not* guaranteed, though. You should work toward a more sustainable business model, then be pleasantly surprised if you hit big.

Learn to love the act of writing, because you'll be doing a *lot* of it. If, deep in your heart, you suspect that you could never reach a point of loving the written word, that you're considering this career and business because the idea of *having written* and the mythical glory that comes with it appeals to you... then maybe find another way to make your millions. There are many less difficult career choices out there.

Time saved: Years, possibly decades.

Don't Make Traditional Publishing Your Base.

How times have changed. Traditional publishing has become the vanity publishing of the modern era.

Back in the dark ages (twenty years ago), vanity publishing was a process where you paid for the printing, blew a lot of money, and ended up with a book with your name on it, while everyone else in the industry eased around you and wrinkled their nose, because vanity publishing was *icky*.

The only plus for you was your name on a volume in your hands.

These days, pursuing a traditional publishing contract will cost you money and time—*years* of it. If you're very, very (*ad infinitum*) lucky, you'll end up with a book with your name on it, and it will be in (some) bookstores, but that's all you get.

You lose all control over that book, forever. You do get an advance, sometimes. However, that's usually the only money you'll see from the book, if your agent doesn't rip you off, and after they've taken their fifteen percent (sometimes twenty). If you compare that advance against the profits you could potentially make publishing it yourself, you're leaving a *lot* of money on the table.

So the only real value in traditionally publishing a book is because you want your name on the cover of a book in the store.

In other words, vanity publishing.

In the time it takes to get a book published with New York, you could have written and released *eight other books* (based on a rate of four books a year), and I'm not even counting the time it takes to land the deal in the first place. Two years is the common lead time from inking the contract to books on shelves.

If it seems to you that I'm dead against traditional for-royalties deals, you're not wrong. However, there are times when taking a traditional New York style deal is worth giving away your book forever.

What I'm suggesting is, don't make traditional publishing your sole business model, because it will break your heart. Establish yourself in the indie world, *first*—which has the side benefit of establishing your author platform, which traditional publishing insists upon before even considering your manuscript.

Then perhaps shop a single title around New York, see if anyone takes a bite. If they do, great! In two years' time, you'll know if you've bought the winning ticket in the lottery. In the meantime, you're still earning indie revenue and paying bills... and building your readership, who will buy the traditionally published title when it is finally released.

Approach traditional publishing with a very clear eye about what you want out of the deal—which can only be intangibles, because New York rarely budges on contract negotiations. Use traditional publishing as a tool to further your career, not their bank balance.

Time saved: Years, possibly decades. Possibly, your life. Check out the publishing road *A Confederacy of Dunces* took, as a good example of the last:

(en.wikipedia.org/wiki/A_Confederacy_of_Dunces)

Don't Switch Genres

Common beginning writer advice: Write what you read.

The only issue with the advice is that most writers are readers, first, and often read dozens of genres and authors. Prolific readers often have eclectic tastes.

When you publish your first title and it doesn't sell as well as you hoped, you'll be tempted to consider that other genre over there, and wonder if you'd do better there.

Or, you'll pick a genre to write in which seems easier to you than the one you really love to read (and which intimidates the bejeesus out of you). Only, once you have one or two books in the "easier" genre under your belt, you start itching about writing a book in your preferred genre.

Or... you plain love *all* the genres and want to roll in all of them like swine in the food trough, sampling everything and loving it all.

Or... you wrote a book in one genre that ended up being way more difficult to write than you suspected it would, while that genre over there looks easier...

Do I speak from experience?

Alas.

All the thought traps I outlined, above, I've fallen into myself, along with a few more. At the time of writing this essay, I am published in six romance sub-genres, science fiction, and non-fiction.

Romance is incredibly stratified, with readers often remaining loyal to their single, narrow sub-genre. They're rabid about that sub-genre. Science fiction isn't quite so bad, but it's getting up there. Just ask any *Star Wars* fan about *Star Trek* novelizations... then take cover.

Genre fiction is by definition a divided territory. That's what makes it work. Readers rarely wander outside their preferred reading aisle. With the development of immortal eBooks and with indie authors pouring more and more books into the genres every day, readers don't *have* to wander to find the next book to read. They can stay right in the middle of their favourite story-land, potentially forever.

When you first set up as an author, pick a genre and stick with it, for at least a whole series (two would be better), before succumbing to the lure of another (sub)genre. I made this mistake and had no idea at the time that I was adding another ten years at least to my "success" path.

I wrote contemporary romance, then tried my hand at a Sherlock Holmes pastiche, then wrote an historical romance, then a romantic suspense, then an erotic romance.

My first contemporary romance sold to a traditional publisher the same week my Sherlock Holmes pastiche did (different publishers). I thought that was a watershed week. It was actually the worst thing that could have happened to me as a brand new author.

Within three months, I'd sold the historical romance to the contemporary romance publisher, and signed the deal on a sequel to the Sherlock Holmes novel with that publisher.

I was over the moon.

Only, I was dividing my readers. Alienating them, in fact. The contemporary romance readers wanted *more contemporary romance*. They ignored the historical romance.

Sherlockian fans... well, they might have been happy with the sequel, only it was released the week of a national postal strike, that lasted two months. The books sat in their printer cartons at the publisher's warehouse. It tanked spectacularly because it never made it into the bookstores in the first place.

The publisher declined to consider a third book in the series, citing "poor sales". (An object lesson in the pitfalls of traditional publishing.)

I figured I was writing in unpopular genres, and got into the new, hot erotic romance business, where I continued to shoot myself in the foot by writing in three different sub-genres *inside* the erotic romance genre.

You'd think I would have figured it out more quickly than I did, but no one talked about branding, series, and genres back then. I had to learn this the hard way, and I'm *still* learning it (because I keep being distracted by another shiny genre over there). Targeting your readers, giving them what they want, book after book, isn't selling out in order to make a buck. It's simple business sense. You do what works, you stop doing what doesn't.

Writing in the same genre (preferably the same series) *works*.

I want to grab that pathetically grateful author signing her first book deals, all those years ago, and shake sense into her. I want to scream at her to *write what you really want and stick with it!*

The time I would have saved! I would have instantly built up my readership (yes, even in traditional publishing). I would have sold more copies with each new release. I would have established myself.

Instead, I bumbled around publishing for years, pleasing no one but my easily distracted inner artist, essentially setting my reader-clock back to zero with every new genre, blindly assuming my loyal fans would follow me anywhere.

Actually, they sort-of did. I have fans who have been with me since I first published. Only, they *just* buy my historical romances. Or they only buy my paranormals. I have plenty of readers that only read a single series I write, but, oh lord, do they *love* that series! (Extra tip: Spin-off series will keep these readers by your side.)

It has taken me fifteen years to reach a point where I have enough readers in each of the (sub)genres to sustain that genre (which also means I must continue to write in it – another pitfall, if you're following a hot genre trend that you don't particularly enjoy writing). I have finally got a clue. I'm *very* careful about targeting and moving beyond genre borders, these days.

I'm not saying you can only ever write in one narrow genre, forever. What I am saying is that you must establish yourself in a genre *first*. Make your name there. Then, *very carefully*, and with full consideration, take on another genre.

And above all, understand that you'll be starting from zero in that genre. Your fans will not cross over just because it is you, not when there are so many other authors in the first genre for them to buy and read. You don't *want* your readers to cross over on Amazon, because they will "pollute" your Also Bought lists, which will depress your sales, almost forever.

Time saved: In my case, around fifteen years and counting. If you stick with one genre at first, you'll likely save yourself years, too.

Don't Fail to Set Up Your Platform as Soon as Possible

I had a website from the get-go. I built it myself with basic HTML, in late 1999. This year, my site turns twenty years old. Now I sell books direct to readers from my site, I run a blog, have a complete and detailed catalogue of all my backlist titles, and the new releases, plus the upcoming releases as pre-orders.

There are well over five hundred pages on the site, and the whole site is a funnel luring readers to sign up for my email list.

Here's a quick timeline to consider:

Late 1999: Built my first site.

March 2015: *Finally* bit the bullet, and built an email list with autoresponders, reader magnets, etc.

December 2015: Quit the day job.

Yes, creating a newsletter list made that much difference.

I cannot over-emphasize this one enough. Between March and December of 2015, my income rose from *ugh* to enough to quit and never look back. The only thing I changed was put a newsletter in place and add some reader magnets to encourage sign-ups. I published the same number of titles, in the same series I'd been writing in for a while.

I didn't start advertising like crazy.

I didn't have a break-though best-seller that raised all other books (I wish!).

I just had a newsletter that I focused upon building for that year, and suddenly, my sales took off enough to match my day job income.

You will find lots of definitions of what author platform is and is not. I define it as simply: *The way you communicate with your readers.*

At a minimum, that is a website where readers can find what books you've published and an email list where you can tell them about the next book you publish. The site supports the email list and not vice-versa.

Social media should be the least priority in your platform. Case in point: I am friends with a best-selling thriller author. He has production deals with Hollywood, a book that is being shopped around to TV production companies like Amazon and Netflix, and thousands upon thousands of fans.

He only communicates with them on Facebook. That's it.

I wince every time I think about how vulnerable he is. Facebook owns his email list. Facebook controls his access to his readers. If Facebook decides to do away with public pages for authors tomorrow, that's it, game over. He's back to zero once more, with the attendant loss in sales.

Your own site and your own email list is a bit of work to establish and more work to keep running, but *you* control it. Research proves that direct email is still the most effective tool for reaching people. Readers open and read email.

Blogging doesn't have nearly the reach. Even in its heyday, it didn't, which is why most bloggers have a supplementary email list, these days.

I've demonstrated the dangers of using social media as your central platform.

I had the site from the beginning, which I guess is kudos to me. Only, I missed the essential bit: I didn't have the email list. For more than fifteen years, I didn't bother, yet it was the key to getting me out of the day-job-from-hell.

Fifteen years!

If only, huh?

Don't do what I did. Or, better still, do what I failed to do. Put your website and email list in place as soon as you can. Capture every reader who likes your books, from day one.

Time saved: Me: Fifteen years.

You: Well, you're not as stupid as me, I hope!

Don't Look for the Magic Bullet

This is a malady that strikes authors once they've got a few books out in the marketplace. The shine of being published has worn off, sales aren't blowing out bank accounts or worse, Hollywood hasn't come calling, or *<insert your long-held dream of publishing success here>*.

Indie publishing is difficult, with thousands of moving parts and a playing field that shifts like the deck of the *Titanic*. It can be bewildering and overwhelming.

Once you've established your fundamentals (books published, platform in place) and you've had a few sales, or even a steady rivulet of cash, you may find yourself wondering what it is you've missed. What have you failed to do that, if you *did* take care of it, would deliver the dream?

This is perhaps one of the hardest things to accept: There is no magic bullet.

There are hundreds of courses and thousands of books out there that purport to have *the* answer, or even *all* the answers, to the mystery of indie publishing success. You can spend every penny you've ever made with your books, and then some more of your personal cash reserves, and still not figure it out.

Still, the promos are alluring, with their promise of answers. They hold out hope.

This is a trap for new and established indie authors, including me. It swallows more than your cash (some of those courses are horribly expensive!) It is a seductive time sink that will slow your rate of success. This seems to be completely counter-intuitive. Courses and books and consultants are supposed to zoom you ahead in your career.

Only, think about what most of those courses and books and consultants ask of you, if you are to derive optimal value from them:

Usually multiple hours of video watching and note-taking, plus…

Exercises to complete and analyse, plus…

A web-community or Facebook page you must join and participate in, and be a good, contributing community member, plus

Extra reading—sometimes whole books of it, often additional blog posts, site pages, and booklets.

Then, after all that sunk time (there is no return on that time investment), you finally get to retool your business along the lines suggested by the teaching resource. This will also involve hours of reorganization, rebuilding, reformatting and more.

Plus, the new tactics and strategies are slower to use, because they're unfamiliar to you. That increases your stress levels, too.

In all that time, have you written anything? Chances are, probably not! As the single most effective indie publishing strategy is getting the next book out, you've lost major income and time.

I speak from experience (again, I say "alas"), when I say these learning resources are the very worst addiction for indie authors, that you must learn to approach the way you would a pissed-off rattlesnake.

Some of the many varied resources and learning tools out there are worth the money and time investment. *Some* of them.

Which ones? It depends, I'm afraid.

This is where having a business framework in place, and your priorities as an indie author engraved in your heart will help you sort out what is a good resources to use and what are just shiny objects that will lure you away from your primary business.

I paid for a very expensive how-to-do-email-marketing course, which paid for itself over and over—it got me out of my day job.

I have paid for courses which teach me how to work with the various advertising platforms, which is an indirect revenue builder, and also an advanced indie strategy (there's no point learning about advertising until you have all your fundamentals in place).

A resource which teaches you how to build your own website might be worth the investment. Or you could pay someone to build it for you—but then you're stuck with paying for all future changes, too. It's a trade off.

The problem with the magic-bullet-style resources is that they promise the world. They imply they will solve all your problems. Sometimes, all they offer behind the rhetoric is a thorough grounding in one tiny aspect of your business (outreach, for example, or how to structure email sequences, or how to build a landing page, or how to make your own audiobooks.).

If you're deficient in that one aspect, and can spare the time, the investment might be worth it.

Do consider if you're grasping at the resource, hoping it will fix all your problems, when a thorough review of your business basics (platform, packaging, story-telling, distribution, etc.) may show gaps that are the *real* cause of low sales, poor ratings, etc.

Slapping a band-aid on a ruptured artery doesn't fix anything, and is often fatal, particularly if you do it frequently.

Here's a way to determine if you're being easily distracted by a magic bullet, or not: Did the resource come to you, or did you go to find it?

Online marketing is *so* effective these days, and the providers of these resources know how to appeal to our deep-seated desires for success. If you tripped across the resource and have been pulled in by the landing page text and the glowing reviews, then there's a good chance this is a shiny object you don't need right now. Before you read the overview of the resource, it's possible you didn't even know this was a thing! Now you're panicking because you haven't been doing xxx all along, and maybe *this* is why you suck as an author?

Don't give in to the guilt-inducing hysteria of promotional materials. Don't let your need for success trip you up. Bookmark the resource and go back to it later, when you determine you need that skill or expertise.

On the other hand, say you've reviewed your business model and decided that you need to expand your distribution by adding audio books to your roster. You search for a resource that will help you do that, and find a course that promises to teach you all you need to know about it. It could be the same course you tripped over six months ago, when you didn't need it. Back then, it was a shiny object. *Now* it is a resource you need, and worth the time and money. You're making an informed decision, not giving into the marketing pitch.

Above all, adopt an experimental mindset.

Determine what skill or tool you might need, based on what you know of your business model right now. Make sure you have baseline data (sales, clicks, engagement—there is a dataset for every occasion). Test the new tool or resource, compare the metrics with your baseline. Worth it, or not? If not, let it go. If yes, do more of it.

Time saved: I have personally succumbed to too many of these shiny object resources over the years. Let's say a couple of years of lost writing time, altogether. You: If you're smart, will save hundreds of hours.

Don't be Afraid

The best for last. This one *still* slays me.

I slid over the statistic, at the very beginning, so you may have missed it. I'll expand it here, just to bring it home.

I wrote my first book when I was fourteen. My English teacher had the secretaries in the front office of my high school type it in manuscript format, and he took it to publishers himself, to see if they were interested. As is the case with most newbie authors, so it was with me: They passed without comment.

However, I was bitten by the writing bug. Hard.

Here's what you might have missed in the introduction, though. Another twenty years passed before I committed to writing for publication.

Why did I wait so long?

There are many answers to that, including psychology, family, the culture I was living in at the time. The biggest, though: Fear.

My fear ran along the lines of: *Who do I think I am, to dare consider writing a book? I'm not like real authors...!*

It took twenty years of self-sabotaging everything else I tried in life, to come back to writing and agree to give it a go. I haven't stopped since.

Are you reading this book because you haven't *quite* got the courage to commit to writing, even though you read compulsively, and you scribble bits of stories when no one is watching?

Do you critique the movies and TV shows you watch, breaking down story structure and character and secretly think: *I wouldn't write it that way...?*

It's possible that fear is stopping you from writing and publishing stories, even though you want to.

Have you published a title or two, learned how hard the business is, and now are wondering if you're a mug for stepping into it in the first place?

A voice whispers, telling you that a life without this frustrating business would be much easier. "Go back to your safe, secure job," it murmurs. No pressure, steady sales cheque, benefits. From here, quitting seems like the only sane thing to do.

That's fear talking. Only, you're reading this book… perhaps hoping to find the encouragement to keep going, or a sliver of an idea for how you might adjust and move on to your version of success.

There are two related ideas which got me through the early years of frustration with the foibles of publishing:

You haven't failed until you quit.

You never know what's around the corner.

The next book you write might find its audience and grow organically, building your career, and letting you quit the day job inside a year.

Or you might add the one missing component to your business model that makes all the difference, as I did with my email list. In February 2015, I would have told you I expected to be in my day job forever.

Time saved: I wasted twenty years pretending I wasn't a writer, because I was afraid.

Yeah… don't do that.

Lessons learned:
- ✓ Don't get into this business unless you really love reading and books.
- ✓ Don't make traditional publishing your base.
- ✓ Don't switch genres.
- ✓ Don't fail to set up your platform as soon as possible.
- ✓ Don't look for the magic bullet.
- ✓ Don't be afraid.

*

Tracy Cooper-Posey is a #1 Best Selling author of romance, science fiction and thrillers. She has published over 100 novels since

1999, been nominated for five CAPAs including Favourite Author, and won the Emma Darcy Award.

Her indie titles have been nominated four times for Book Of The Year, won in 2012, and awarded a SFR Galaxy Award in 2016. She has been a national magazine editor and taught writing at MacEwan University for a decade.

An Australian Canadian, Tracy lives in Edmonton, Canada with her husband, a former professional wrestler, where she moved in 1996 after meeting him online.

Learn more about her at https://TracyCooperPosey.com

Baby, I was Born This Way
James A. Owen

I've often remarked that everyone must find their own path to their goals, and every path is going to be different. Sharing the details of one's own path can be helpful, but not as a map to follow in every detail. Conditions change. The market changes. The path followed by one person will never appear in the exact same way to another. But to simply know that it *is* possible to walk a difficult path and reach an important goal has value. And knowing how someone else overcame the specific challenges they faced can be of immense help to someone who may simply just be trying to decide how to get started.

Some of us began walking the path to our goals almost before we even knew there *was* a path. Or goals.

What I am most known for is the book *Here, There Be Dragons*, which has been published in more than twenty languages around the world, and which remains in print in hardcover after nearly thirteen years. It was published by Simon & Schuster, known as one of the "Big Five" in traditional publishing. But I actually began my career in publishing at the lofty age of six, writing and illustrating little picture books which I sold to the neighbors around the block for fifteen cents each.

*

I was raised in a family of artists, and drew my inspiration for my creative work, as well as my aspirations for a viable career in the arts, from them. My mother was a first-grade teacher, who also painted, but more significantly, also created all of the art and designs for her lesson plans herself. She taught me about narrative, and how to use visuals in teaching and storytelling, and how to make use of the materials I had available.

Her older brothers were printers, and the elder of the two was also a painter who specialized in Native American Kachina dancers. Together with his oldest daughter, he created a series of coloring books based on his paintings, which were among the first artistic memories I have.

I grew up surrounded by images of men and women and children dressed in bright clothing which was covered in beads and feathers, and who often had wings, and the heads of animals and birds. My cousin was only a few years older than I was, and her paintings and work on the coloring books taught me that the creations and contributions of a child could be just as valid and meaningful and valued as those of an adult.

And my mother's younger sister was a graphic designer who took me as her apprentice when I was only thirteen, and who taught me about presentation, and working with clients, and precision in my work. I learned how to create logos from her, and how to shape an artistic identity. The first company logo I was allowed to try my hand at – for a company called Hatch Construction and Paving – was selected out of several proposed designs, and which is still in use today. (And more than three decades after that job, I was honored when the company president asked me to design the logo for their new company, Hatch Concrete, as well. The first time I got a hamburger from my aunt. I was better paid the second time.)

All of these influences inspired the crayon-drawn and hand-stapled editions of *Goldilocks and the Three Bears* and *Little Red Riding-Hood* (both also featuring Santa Claus) which I produced in extremely limited editions, in a sales region that was limited to our block, since I wasn't allowed to cross the street. (Much like in the grown-up world though, there were some violations of this guideline, but they were allowed at the time, possibly because when I went to the corner grocery store to buy a sparking ray gun with my earnings, I also bought my mom a container of her favorite sunflower seeds. This may or may not be the most significant lesson in this essay.)

*

I elevated my ambitions and activities to a more professional level when I was sixteen, as a publisher and exhibitor at the San Diego Comic-Con, with the debut of my first comic book, *Pryderi Terra*. I used all the skills I had learned from my various family members in the creation, design, and execution of this magazine-sized, black and white fantasy comic book. But as with most things, especially in publishing, stuff slips through. Errors occur.

The small piece of acetate with the company logo, issue number, and price which I had meticulously attached to the top of the cover art, fell *off.* Ten thousand comic books were printed and bound with no issue designation or price on the cover. So, after we picked them up in a rented U-Haul – which my aunt drove, since I didn't have a license yet – we stopped at an office supply store and bought ten thousand little white round sticky tabs. At the hotel in San Diego, we wrote $1.75 on all the stickers and affixed them to enough copies to cover all of the orders we hoped to fulfill at the convention.

I had chosen a paper stock I thought looked good, but which was, for a comic book, way too high in quality and – correspondingly and unsurprisingly – in price. At wholesale, which was how I hoped to move most of the copies, I would be *losing* five cents per copy. That's not really an effective way to build a business, unless you have a *lot* of capital, which I didn't.

I had printed up some really nice, folded 7" x 7" promotional flyers, but had neglected to include any contact information whatsoever. (But I did have a rubber stamp with my company name and address, and business cards as well, so that one was a pass.)

And despite all of these little/big issues and instances where things went wrong, I also did a lot of things right. At the trade show portion of the event, I arranged a private presentation for the association of distributors, and I could speak and present well. I could articulate my plans. And I had copies of a comic printed on really nice paper to hand out to them to evaluate for their catalogs. (I still have relationships with many of those people today.)

At the convention part of the week, where the goal was to sell to consumers, my aunt, my partner Jimmy, and my friend Bryan and I proudly displayed our books and prints on a table and standing displays Jimmy and I had built in my mom's barnyard. (Though the floor manager *did* make us take down the nice drapery we had hand-sewn, because it was flammable.)

The second or third day, a quiet, small little Filipino man named Fil hung around the booth and asked questions about my book. I'd seen him trying to talk to other vendors, some of whom responded, while others did not. But I liked him, and I was grateful for his interest in my comic. He contacted me after the show and asked if he could order some copies – then he ordered more than most of the distributors combined.

Fil, it turned out, owned the largest chain of pop culture stores in the Philippines – and I achieved best-seller status for the first time (selling second only to *X-Men* that month in his stores) because he had copies in volume, liked my art, and recommended me to his customers.

I learned a lot because of those experiences, and while I had planned for – and promoted – what was now *The Chronicles of Pryderi Terra* to be an ongoing series, my art was improving in great leaps, and so I kept revising the second issue. It only ever saw print as an extended preview in the trade newspaper, *The Comics Buyer's Guide*, but the important thing is that it did see print – and in a venue where many, many thousands more readers would see it.

My career in comics took a pause for several years while I did other things – like finish high school – but I kept my hand in both art and design, doing lots of corporate identity design and commercial illustration. I also tried to propose some comics projects to a number of publishers – a graphic adaptation of *Silas Marner* for First Comics' Classics Illustrated line, and a Superman project I called *Star Child* (the translation of his name, *Kal El*, in Kryptonese), but those did not take hold for various reasons.

*

Then, in my early twenties, circumstances had made it possible for me to choose to get back into comics again full time. I was married then, and my wife and I started a new publishing company, with the intent to produce a fantasy comic book series that repurposed my unused *Silas Marner* pages and the energy and title from the Superman proposal. I called it *StarChild*.

We needed to sell at least a thousand copies just to pay the printing bill for the first issue. We listed it in the distributor catalogs, and we got back orders for twelve hundred copies. All good. Then the orders for the second issue came in at half that amount, which would have been a problem if it hadn't been take over a week later by a bigger problem: I crushed my drawing hand in a car accident.

I detail the events of those days in my book and lecture *Drawing out the Dragons*, but for the purposes of this essay only one choice matters: I decided my career was not over, and I was going to find a way to continue.

I created *StarChild #0* as a prequel to the other issues, and I did the half-page layouts for it with my left hand. Then, I approached other artists I had met in my *Pryderi Terra* days and asked them to ink the art so the book could be published –and some of the greatest artists in the trade responded, in part because of my story, but also because they remembered and respected that nervously confident teenager from the San Diego Comic-Con. We listed it in the catalogues...

...and we got orders for more than forty-five thousand copies.

That book was one of the best-selling independent comic books of the season. By the time it came out, my hand had healed, and I could draw issue three, which sold seventeen thousand copies. The distributors reordered enough copies of the first two issues we had to go into new printings. I was invited to go on a convention tour and exhibit at trade shows with other well-known cartoonist publishers. The combined sales of the issues of *StarChild* that we published eventually reached into the hundreds of thousands.

My career rose higher and higher. I was approached by someone who was a fan of my comics (who was, in fact, a well-known author in Europe) to write some novels for a German publisher – the origin of my *MythWorld* novels – and spun the comics publishing into magazines as well – the two-volume, slipcased journal *Argosy*, which lost money in amounts correspondingly proportional to the design awards it won; and *International Studio*, the oversized arts magazine which actually *did* make money. And then... my magazine distributor went under, and I was left with lots of debt, and no way to even begin to pay it, short of my two-part plan: to write and sell a bestselling novel, and then get a movie deal for a gazillion dollars.

Which brings us back full circle to *Here, There Be Dragons*.

*

The book deal which I eventually landed at a Big Five mainstream traditional publisher did indeed result in a bestselling novel; and the concurrent movie deal, while not for a gazillion dollars, was substantial enough to breathe new life into my career and, well, *me*.

Part of the reason I opted to sign with Simon & Schuster as opposed to other publishers was because they agreed to let me illustrate both the book *and* the cover. That is an unusual thing to cede to a novelist – but the samples I showed them, as well as the track record I had with other published work, convinced them.

We went through a few different designs before we settled on the finished piece, and the contributions of my own apprentices and the art director all combined into a cover that won a gold medal at the New York Book Awards.

But that isn't the most meaningful victory of having done the cover.

My publisher wanted to launch the book with a cross-country book tour, starting in Manhattan. I asked that the very first signing be at a comic book store called Jim Hanley's Universe. They were confused by this request – to sign at a store they really didn't have on their bookselling radar at all – but as I was doing other signings in traditional bookstores too, they saw no harm in saying yes.

For my part, I simply wanted to do it as a show of loyalty and gratitude to the market that had given me my career to that point. Also, the store manager, my friend Vito, was really excited to host a big book signing.

The day of the event, my editor and publicist called and said that several comic book stores in the city were carrying *Here, There Be Dragons*. I thought that was great – but they didn't really understand why that was happening. They hadn't marketed the book to those stores in particular, and so couldn't understand why they were stocking the book.

I explained that I had relationships with all those store owners going back fifteen years to my *StarChild* days and earlier, in some cases, and so I had let them know about the book. I knew that all of the other sales channels were well in hand with the publisher, so I wasn't as worried about doing anything there – and besides, I'd been told when I signed the contract to tone down my enthusiasm for promotion, because there were other people at the publisher who did that so I wouldn't have to.

(I did it anyway, at least to the comic book shops, because I essentially needed to sell enough books for that sparking ray gun, so to speak, and Ii thought bringing some sunflower seeds to the table in the form of supportive stores couldn't hurt.)

At the signing, which was well-attended, the first person in line stepped forward and put an enormous stack of books and comics in front of me. It contained copies of *Pryderi Terra* (with a round sticker on the front that read $1.75), the issue of *The Comics Buyer's Guide* with the unpublished second issue in it, every issue of *StarChild*, the *StarChild* paperbacks, the limited edition hardcovers, and five copies of *Here, There Be Dragons*.

My editor asked what it was that interested him in a young adult fantasy novel, and he replied that to him, it wasn't a young adult fantasy novel, it was a new book by James Owen. He had been buying my work, at that store, since my first published comic – and if the store continued to carry my novels, he'd buy all of those there, too.

My publicist turned to my editor and quipped, "I'm really glad we let him do the cover."

That book has since been through more than a dozen printings in hardcover and nearly as many in paperback. There are seven sequels, many of which have also been translated into other languages. There are omnibus editions, and many ancillary products like coloring books, prints, t-shirts, and other related books – all of which have and are being published, as when my career started, by my own imprint.

*

The books I am best known for are the traditionally-published novels; but what began, established, and is now furthering my career are the books I am publishing myself. Each supports the other – but before I became a traditionally published author, I had a long, long, career in publishing that I began entirely on my own.

And this, *this*, is the heart of everything, the white-hot, burning core of this essay: In life, all of your choices are cumulative. Each choice you make informs and becomes a part of all of your future choices. The better your choices are, on average, the better your life can be.

It's much the same in publishing.

All of the decisions you make about your work are cumulative – and the sooner you make the decision that your work is worthy of being seen, the sooner that becomes the reality. Now, more than ever before, we exist in a market that is shaped by visibility. Work that isn't seen cannot be valued. And often, too many writers and artists of talent and potential wait for indications from others that their work has value.

Don't misunderstand: that is pretty much the way of traditional publishing. You wait for responses from agents, who wait for responses from editors, then you wait again for publishing dates.

Traditional publishing, for all its benefits, is largely a waiting game. And it is not always one that pays off. Manuscripts can languish for years, before circumstances change for good... or for ill. Careers wait, hoping for the validation that may or may not come, and in the meantime, calendar pages that you never get back are flipping past with greater and greater speed.

I owe a great deal to traditional publishing. But I also think I've demonstrated before and since that getting a traditional deal was never going to be the only path I followed in order to bring my work to the world. I was always a storyteller; I was always an entrepreneur. I was always going to find some way to print and distribute the work I created. And in this increasingly interconnected world, it is becoming easier and easier to do.

Bear in mind, I'm not talking about issues of relative quality.

The first comic I did was pretty rough, ditto in large part for the first couple of issues of *StarChild*. My first novel, the second *MythWorld* (which was written before the first) was too short, and needed beefing up.

If any of those creative works had been subject to the traditional publishing path, they would probably have been rejected outright, or at been subject to significant revision before anyone published them. (The *MythWorld* editor was a fan of my writing already, and gently worked me through the changes I need before the publisher ever saw it.)

Even now, the best advice I give to anyone planning to self-publish is to hire competent professionals to help you: get a pro cover artist and designer, and a freelance editor with solid references. The basics of the quality of publishing are still important, and with my early works, it wasn't that I ignored those basics so much as that I didn't really know better. I was using my own judgment, and in that judgment the work was professional enough, quality enough, to publish, and begin a career with.

Would those early books and comics have been better? Possibly. But again, the path I followed was not conventional or easy. If I had held off publishing *StarChild* until it was "better," then maybe I would not have had the accident – which resulted in the book that launched by career in earnest, nor would I have gotten the attention of the editor who proposed *MythWorld*.

Instead, I grew with the work, and improved as I created it – and in doing so, built a name and a body of work that sustains me even now.

Every time I sell a *StarChild* volume, I'm making money off of work that I created half a lifetime ago. It wasn't as good as my work is now, but that the way of all things. It's as good as I could do then, and that was good enough to publish and charge money for, and that's all that matters.

There has been a fear, voiced by many new and aspiring authors, that traditional publishers, editors, and agents don't want to even consider buying a manuscript which has been published in any form. I think that approach is being replaced by a publishing viewpoint that considers a broader set of criteria for establishing value – value which has to begin with the creator, first. If you value what you do, then others will begin to also.

And if you demonstrate the belief in the value of your work by publishing it yourself, then, at minimum, you will have gained valuable insights into the process, your market, and your creative abilities. At best, you will have begun to build a body of work for yourself, and a name that carries a value of its own. The market will recognize that. And so will readers, and editors, and agents, and your peers, who are traveling to the same place on different paths.

I was once asked how I got my first lucky break. I replied that I chiseled it myself, out of stone, and then when I needed another, I did it again.

Ask yourself, how bad do I want it? How much would I give, how much would I do, to reach my goals? In publishing, if your answer depends too much on the input and evaluation of others, then they will control your career, your output, and your precious calendar days.

But if your answer is based entirely on your own valuation of your work, then no one else's opinions will really matter. They simply become a part of the overall plan for the path you've chosen to walk. Then, you will finally understand: it's not about goals; it's about the process of reaching them. Goals can change, and if you fail to reach the ones you set, then you find yourself at the base of the mountain again, starting over.

But if your life, and work, and career becomes about the process, then as goals change and obstacles arise, you can shift to accommodate whatever needs to be done in order to keep making progress.

In the end, your career becomes about two things: doing good work, and making sure it is seen. Those two things are entirely in your power to make happen. Make good work, consistently, and you can make a living. Do it for long enough, and then your name alone represents the quality of work that you do. Are you good enough? There's only one way to be sure – do the work, and show it to the world. Then do it again.

That's all there really is. It's just that simple. It's just that hard. And I wouldn't trade it for anything.

Lessons learned:
- ✓ As with most things, especially in publishing, stuff slips through. Errors occur.
- ✓ Be polite and courteous to everyone – a great deal of success in this industry comes from the relationships you develop

✓ When things go wrong – and they often will – find a way to continue.

✓ In life, all of your choices are cumulative. Each choice you make informs and becomes a part of all of your future choices. The better your choices are, on average, the better your life can be.

✓ The sooner you make the decision that your work is worthy of being seen, the sooner that becomes the reality

✓ It's not about goals; it's about the process of reaching them, as goals change and obstacles arise, you can shift to accommodate whatever needs to be done in order to keep making progress

✓ Do the work, and show it to the world. Then do it again

*

James A. Owen is founder and executive director of Coppervale International, an art and design studio that also published the periodicals International Studio *and* Argosy, *develops television and film projects, and among other ventures, is redesigning an entire town in Arizona.*

James has written and illustrated the massive Essential StarChild *graphic novel, the award-winning* MythWorld *series of novels, the bestselling series* The Chronicles of the Imaginarium Geographica, *the inspirational nonfiction book* Drawing out the Dragons, *and more. More than a million copies of his publications are in print, and are sold all over the world.*

With a Little Help From my Friends

John M. Olsen

I wrote my first piece of fiction intended for sale in 1994, submitted it to *Internet World* magazine, and they accepted it. It was a total fluke for several reasons.

First, *Internet World* didn't publish fiction.

Second, I knew almost nothing about story structure.

Third, I knew very little about the publishing industry which contributed to my ignorance on points one and two. I got lucky in part because my story was a modern-day retelling of *A Christmas Carol* with a theme of internet flame wars. I borrowed an already-solid story and put my own words into that structure.

Still, I was a published author, and that let me check a box on my bucket list. Someone had paid me actual money for a story I'd written. I'd been an avid reader since my early teens, absorbing my father's library of science fiction, fantasy, action adventure, and other genres. I saw those books on the shelf and thought it would be the coolest thing ever to write books like the ones those authors wrote. My heroes included Andre Norton and Isaac Asimov among several other greats in the industry.

After my one-hit-wonder sale, life made demands for my attention. For about the next twelve years I concentrated on my family and a career in software development, moving three times and changing jobs several times. Technology can be volatile. Software ramps that volatility up a little. Then for a few years I wrote code for the games industry, which is the most volatile of all software jobs. I've done well professionally, and enjoyed working in the software industry, even through those volatile years, but eventually I felt a draw to carve out some time and get back into writing.

*

In 2007 I wrote and submitted four short stories. One was accepted and put into a "we might use this later" folder. They paid me for it, so I got a second taste of that dangling carrot of success. Looking back on those stories, the other three had issues. The publishers were right to toss them and send me polite rejections.

Once again, work and family took control, and life got busy. More time passed.

*

In 2013 a coworker told me about a small press with regular open calls to a series of anthologies they were publishing. Each had a theme, and the themes sounded like a lot of fun. Fantasy, Paranormal, and this new thing called Steampunk, all sounded like a lot of fun to experiment with. I figured I'd give it a shot and entered stories into each contest as they were announced.

Here's where the first major plot twist appears.

By this time, I had a small support group of friends who knew something about the publishing industry. While my first three tries ended in rejections, the fourth was accepted, in part due to feedback from my friends, and Xchyler Publishing agreed to put my story *Revolutionary* into their *Steel & Bone* steampunk anthology.

That by itself would have been great, but this would be no ordinary edit pass. The editor, Penny Freeman, was out to find new authors who showed promise, and the authors going into that collection each got what I can now identify as a master class on short story editing. She ran my story through the wringer. Penny helped me analyze plot points, adjust flow, correct wording, and a host of other tweaks that the spelling and grammar checker in Microsoft Word could never understand.

I began to see what I'd done well by accident, and I worked to do it on purpose as I added new skills to my writing toolbox. It's a lot like cleaning out a cluttered storage unit. You don't see the little disorganized piles of junk until you throw out the broken couches and dead mattresses that hide the smaller problems. Eventually, you get down to the dust bunnies lurking in the corners.

One of my rejections from Xchyler later found its way to be an Honorable Mention in a DragonComet writing competition, and after applying my newly-discovered skills, another sold to an online publication. I was on my way.

Behind all my efforts, my group of friends supported me—once they saw my persistence and willingness to learn from those around me. They told me about a writing conference, and I figured I would show up and see what I could learn at the *Life, the Universe, and Everything* writing symposium in Provo, Utah.

Mind blown.

Not only did I not know what I was doing, I barely had the language to form questions to take me to the next step. I heard of several story structure templates, then I learned how they all mirror each other and merely focus on different aspects of the same basic structure. I integrated all this new information into my writing, and my short stories improved.

I met more writers and became friends with more kindred spirits. As a lifelong introvert, this took me well outside my comfort zone, and this was an important part of my education as a writer.

The thing about a comfort zone is that it is a non-learning zone as well. We have to try new ideas and learn new skills to improve. My career in software gave me a great background in analysis, and I applied it with gusto to writing. Learning became an integral part of my writing, as I applied all the new ideas I learned. I knew I couldn't get where I wanted to go with writing unless I set up a parallel focus on learning. Attending conferences became a regular thing.

*

In 2015 I tried NaNoWriMo (National Novel Writing Month), where authors work to write 50,000 words in November. I had written a fictionalized biography some time before to meet a promise to a family member, so I knew I could write that many words in a single story. I can look back at that biography now and cringe at its lack of editing, but it gave me confidence on tackling a bigger project.

I jumped into the deep end of the pool, and my first fantasy novel, *Crystal King*, was born. I didn't finish the whole thing that November, but I hit around 60,000 words, then finished it over the next few months. I submitted it to Immortal Works, a local small press, in August 2016. They didn't require an agent which meant I had to apply my analytical skills and a lot of research to understand the inner workings of the contract they sent me.

Meanwhile, I kept writing new short stories across several genres, mostly tied to science fiction and fantasy. A friend I had met at writing events had such a large backlist of short stories that she often had twenty or thirty out for submission at once. With her inspiration driving me, I figured I would see how hard I could push with short story submissions.

I set myself two major goals for 2017:

First, I worked to hit a new high on total short stories out for submission. I sent out each story to just one market at a time, which is the industry standard, so I was gong to need a lot of stories to hit my goal. At first I struggled to get two or three out at a time.

Second, I addressed the problem of receiving rejections. This is often the most discouraging part of writing, so I decided to turn it into a game where I kept score with my rejections. Some authors tell stories of stacking them up or collecting them on a spike, but I did one better. I decided that I wanted to receive thirty short story rejections that year. It seemed like a modest, achievable goal that would force me into new territory.

To receive that many rejections, I had to keep my stories out on the market. When one came back with a rejection, I had to send the story back out as soon as possible. If someone accepted one of my stories for publication, that reduced my pool of circulating stories, forcing me to keep writing to keep the pipeline full. My rejection goal motivated me.

At one point I had twenty-nine rejections and I received an email from a publisher. In eager anticipation, I figured it would either be another acceptance or it would push me over the top of my goal. Either option was great. I was running at about a twenty percent acceptance rate by that time, so I couldn't predict the outcome, but statistically, I expected it to be a rejection.

I opened the email, and found the publisher wanted to hold my story for further consideration. Not an acceptance. Not a rejection. My story hung in limbo, and I still sat at twenty-nine rejections. The year wasn't over yet, so I pressed on.

By the end of the year, I topped my goal with thirty-six rejections; and at my high point I had ten stories out circulating at one time. Those are piker numbers compared to my friend Julie, but for me it was an amazing experience. I sold six short stories in 2017 during my rejection exercise.

I learned several things that year. Besides improving basic skills by writing so many new stories, I began to apply those lessons to my novel-in-progress. I learned about short story markets and learned who accepted what kind of story. On top of my writing skills, I learned more about organizing my time, setting goals, and achieving them.

*

I discovered an interesting side effect the coming year. Because of my new industry contacts, my networking with other authors, and my improved skills, I ended up selling nine stories and receiving only twelve rejections the following year. My success ratio on submissions rose from about fifteen percent in 2017 to over forty percent in 2018.

Having appeared in several anthologies at this point, I had a new first. An editor *invited me* to participate in a new anthology. This would have never happened without my big push to get my work out there in front of the eyeballs of editors.

I should explain one of my goals with short stories. While it's theoretically possible to make a meager living on short stories, the practicalities of it are that you don't write short stories to generate a significant income. Whether I get a onetime payment or royalties on sales, I rarely get more than enough to occasionally super-size my fast food meal when I eat out.

Rather than hoping to roll in piles of cash, my goals were more humble. I used stories to get my name out there, in front of the right people. Editors and other authors got to know me. I share tables of contents with dozens of authors now, and I've attempted to get to know as many as possible.

While going through all this work on short stories, I wrote *Crystal Queen*, the second book in my fantasy trilogy. Along with book two, I wrote a prequel short story to give away to readers as a marketing tool. The short story includes links to the novel.

One thing to understand about publishers, and small press in particular, is that most marketing efforts rely heavily upon the author. Marketing was an area I found myself short on information, so I added it to my list of things to learn. I still feel like I'm barely learning the words to form the right questions with marketing, but I've started down the path.

Just like with writing, I've found plenty of people willing to help me learn how to market both my novels and my short stories. I've discovered online groups to follow, and expanded my list of contacts. I've expanded my pool of friends to include not just authors, but several editors. That's amazing when I look at my natural introvert tendencies. I've learned over the past few years to pretend to be an extrovert for long enough stretches to accomplish quite a bit with actual social interactions.

*

Several other things changed as I got to know more people and built my skill set. Rather than just attending conferences, I proposed classes. This led to opportunities to teach beginning and aspiring authors, and to rub elbows with other panelists.

An interesting thing happens when you post on social media about conferences and include links to all the panelists and speakers. Their friends show up to comment. I hadn't expected this response for some reason, but it worked out great because I have always been positive in my reviews and posts tied to the events I attend. I always assume the people I talk about will see what I say, and I don't want to sound like a jerk.

(Basic professionalism is a subject I don't have time for here, but it's a requirement if you want to be seen as a professional author.)

Once again, my circle of contacts expanded, with no sign of slowing. Since that time, I've joined a professional writing association and served in a leadership capacity, working with – and learning from – writers at all levels.

Looking back, nearly every step in the process has been self-inflicted. I've never been one to sit idly by. Not only do I inflict new learning opportunities on myself, I do it in new areas that may or may not have a connection to skills I already possess.

At a recent conference I learned yet another new idea: If you don't have the vocabulary to talk about a concept, you probably don't understand the concept. We have to learn to talk about ideas before those ideas can take root and grow. Learning how to learn is more important than learning any given skill because it gives you the tools to control, aim, and accelerate your progress.

*

As you can tell, I'm passionate about the concept of creation as a whole, and writing in particular. The idea that there are new concepts waiting for me drives me forward. I want to reemphasize a concept that's easy to miss. There is a whole world of information out there where we don't know enough yet to even ask the right questions. Part of my quest is to learn the questions, then learn whatever is hiding behind those questions.

I've turned in the third book in my fantasy trilogy now, which means *Crystal Empire* should come out about two years after book one was released. I'm up to twenty-three short story sales, and have a lot of other projects in the works. Where I sit now is entirely due to the combination of my choices to get involved, and the support I've received at every step from friends, family, and the local writing community.

Just like the Beatles, I get by with a little help from my friends.

Will your journey look like mine? Not by a long shot.

Will there be the occasional parallel? Almost certainly. What I hope others can glean from my experience is the occasional nugget to draw upon, rather than trying to follow in my every footstep.

I wouldn't wish my odd path on anyone, but it has worked for me. Each person and each path is unique, even if they lead to a similar place. I'll see you there.

Lessons learned
- ✓ Get out of your comfort zone and jump in with both feet.
- ✓ Spend time doing what you love on the schedule you are happy with.
- ✓ Network, network, network!
- ✓ Sometimes you won't even know the questions to ask. This can be fixed with study and effort.
- ✓ Support from writer-aware friends makes a difference.

*

John M. Olsen edits and writes speculative fiction across multiple genres, and loves stories about ordinary people stepping up to do extraordinary things. He hopes to entertain and inspire others with his award-winning stories as he passes his passion on to the next generation of avid readers. He loves to create and fix things, whether editing or writing novels or short stories or working in his secret lair equipped with dangerous power tools.

In all cases, he applies engineering principles and processes to the task at hand, often in unpredictable ways.

A Late Start
is Never "Too Late"
V. Castro

Its 2017 and life is plodding along, as it does when you reach a certain age or decide to start a family. A year had passed since my husband and I began trying to conceive our second child (my third) without any luck. Although life was good in all the ways society measures success, I felt incomplete. Happy, but something inside of me was stalled. There were days I felt locked in a waking sleep paralysis (parental sleep deprivation doesn't help!).

How can an incredible amount of love and emptiness reside in the same body?

Since becoming a stay-at-home mother, my self-esteem resembled a two sizes two small sweater full of holes eaten by moths year after year. Yes, I am very privileged to have witnessed amazing firsts in my children's lives; however, that doesn't make the 24/7 wheel of stay-at-home parenthood any less exhausting or isolating. The days are both long and short. There never seems to be enough time in the day to complete all those child-centric household tasks, but at the same time, the clock moves *so* slowly as I wait for my husband to come home and provide me with some respite.

Since I wasn't pregnant, we decided to enjoy a weekend away in Lake Como, Italy. It's a short, inexpensive flight from London, and had been a dream destination all my life. As long as I could still eat unpasteurized cheese and drink wine, why not?

We spent the evenings sipping wine until midnight. One night, slightly tipsy, I remember seeing clouds cover the moon until it morphed into a yellow cat's eye. It was like an ominous omen right in front of me. I decided to grab the universe by the collar: "Lord, you got a minute? I need your help. I'm running on empty"

It's funny, I always wanted to write. I devoured books as a child, always loving the library. I gravitated towards books about history or tales on the slightly spooky side. *Scary Stories To Tell In The Dark* by Alvin Schwartz will always be hands down one of my favourite series to read.

Recently my mother gave me folders filled with "books" I had written. One happens to be a vampire story I penned at nine years old. In my twenties my friends and I joked all the shenanigans we got up to would be going in "The Book." Whenever I travelled, I saw stories unfolding in these locations with characters I could almost see. However, they were odd shape pieces to different puzzles. Nothing compelled me to sit down and write.

When we returned from Como, it was back to the laundry, groceries, school run, cooking routine. Then one morning I awoke from a dream that would end up being book two in my series. Without hesitation, I dusted off my computer (and brain) and began to write the bones of my tale with an invigoration I had not felt in ages. Who the hell knew you could send a prayer into the universe and get a reply?

I wrote non-stop and it felt so good as everything seemed to just flow. This was something just for me. Every minute was bliss. However, I was too shy to say anything to anyone. No one knew until it became too obvious to hide from my husband. Even on the weekends I wanted nothing but to allow this vision to pour out of me.

Right when I thought I knew where it was going, a story within a story emerged. I was listening to the song *Maria Maria* by Santana while writing an intimate moment between two characters, and in that moment, Maria was born.

I continued to write, but couldn't get this minor character out of my head. She was only meant to show the humanity still left in another character, a bit of backstory. But the more I wrote, the more her personality formed in my mind. Maria was a bad ass waiting to kick open the door of my imagination and escape. My original idea would now be a series centered around this Mexican woman.

Horror is dominated by white males. I wanted to challenge that. I wanted to see a character that represented *my* background. This book was going to be about different women in different times in history, assigned to places not by their choosing. I wanted to watch them break free and be something more than what they were told was their only place in the world. The fire that was a small pile of kindling now blazed.

I'd viciously peddle on a spin bike with dialogue darting between my ears. I could see Maria's face, hear her voice... and suddenly my world was no longer flat, but round with lots of strange things lurking in dark corners. When it was time to pick up my son from the gym I'd write on my iPhone as he romped in the soft play.

Maria and her story flew out of me in two months. I tried to write the second book at the same time, but too many competing ideas would not allow the focus I needed. Instead, I took a few days to dump all of my vision for all books onto my computer. I felt good about myself again.

Then the thing we had waited for finally happened. Now there were two babies: one inside my belly and one on my laptop.

*

Maria The Wanted was shaping up as a novella. It needed so much work. Through a chance meeting a few months earlier, I was introduced to a woman that also happened to be a literary agent. I reached out for feedback. She gave me excellent advice which I heeded, but didn't really understand until I got it in my mind that I might have a go in the publishing world.

I was starting to feel mildly better into my second trimester, and went from 30k to 90k words writing everyday while my children were in school. I went over and over and over my manuscript. My entire focus was on the book. Come on agents, I'm here!!

My husband, being the business-minded person he is, thought self-publishing was the way forward from the outset, but I guess I needed validation. I wanted to know if there was any merit in this project. I needed assurance, but could only bear showing it to complete strangers. My husband is incredibly supportive of my writing, but he absolutely *hates* anything that resembles horror. No wares, vampires, shifters, zombies, demons or monsters. So showing my book to him wasn't going to work, even though he's great with business advice or taking care of the children so I could write.

Then began the process of querying and editing.

All that querying advice you read about is real. Ignore at your peril. There wasn't anything out there in the adult horror/fantasy book world too similar to my main character, so I thought, how hard could it be?

Folks, always do your homework!

I always loved reading, but homework not so much. The publishing game is no joke. Remember that publishing is a for profit industry. They will do what they think will lead to selling books. Research every avenue in publishing.

I was surprised how many agents gave me some feedback. It was so greatly appreciated. Of course, their feedback also came with rejection after rejection.

At first, I didn't mind the rejections. It was exhilarating to have something of my own. I was rediscovering who I was before children. But slowly, the worse I felt in my pregnancy, the worse the climate of my mind became. Depression cut through me like a recently sharpened samurai sword. This hadn't happened during my previous pregnancies nor had I experienced post-natal depression either. I can be a salty, stubborn woman, but not this down. What was happening to me?

I'd cry after the school run and when my husband left for work. I'd had such high hopes for my book. I felt so good about this tale I was weaving. I wanted to see a strong Latina have her own platform. We are so rarely seen or heard.

Let me tell you, sending queries from a different time zone than your prospective agents is not so fun. I ate rejection for breakfast. It wasn't the form rejections that got me, it was the ones with personal notes. The ones that said, "So close, but just not right for my list." "Great concept, but not for me at the moment," or the worst, "I know an agent will represent you soon."

Would that be the story of my life? I already felt completely inadequate in my home life and now this. Was I worthy of anything except being a glorified housekeeper Intellectually and in my heart I knew this wasn't true, however, those were the emotions brewing inside of me. There is nothing worse than a deep sadness invading the tiny crevices of your cells and refusing to budge no matter how hard you will it to go.

My husband was always so supportive, reminding me that I'm a great mother and all of this would pass. Until he reads this, I don't think he ever knew how many whirlpools swirled inside, causing me to feel like I was drowning most of the time.

Looking back, I sent the manuscript out way too early.

Don't ever underestimate the power that is editing. You would not believe how many times one's eyes cannot see that missing period ten times in a row. When you think you've edited enough...... Nope. Do like Britney. Hit me baby one more time! Eventually I paid to have my query and first pages looked over. Money well spent, too.

After the edit, I got more responses, more glimmers of hope, but that was all. Tiny specks of hope that shined at the moment but were just a mirage of what I wanted so desperately.

At this point, my back was killing me with every step and the English weather permanently in Groundhog Day like dreariness. I was ill with a different virus every week (a three year old's gift that keeps on giving). And if you've ever had the flu while heavily pregnant, honey you haven't lived. I'd look on with envy as my husband and children gulped down medicine as I settled for hot tea. Most cold medicines are not suitable during pregnancy.

I felt betrayed by my body. I hated my unhappiness, my stupidity for thinking I could write. The inner dialogue kept repeating what an ungrateful witch I was. I was healthy, my baby and children healthy, I wanted for nothing. But that mental voice kept screaming, "Cry me a damn river!" More sobbing with headphones as I watched it rain day after day.

Self-flagellation is worse than rejection.

I had to write. It was my only escape from what I was feeling. I stopped sending out queries and began writing short stories. This didn't mean I gave up on my series. More ideas kept popping up like a game of Whack-a-Mole that I couldn't resist delving into. I told myself to shut-the-fuck-up and get on with it. Smile dammit. You'll have a daughter soon and you owe it to her to be a good example.

Up to my daughter's birth I was revising, sending out queries and manuscript requests. And then there was the waiting. Waiting to have my child or hear back from the universe. Which would come first?

*

One of the manuscript requests had asked about my platform. It hadn't seemed important before - for me, it was all about the story, the character. Surely the story is enough, right?

Nope. Wrong again.

So I decided that while I was waiting it was time to start building an author's platform and not just think about it. At least now I had a product in my hands and more in my head. I had something I could promote.

Now, I always liked Facebook because my husband and I are alone in London, and it kept me in touch with my family and old school friends that live abroad. And I was on Instagram because my younger sisters were on it. At that point I only used Twitter for agent/editor pitch parties – which are great when you get likes. Surprisingly, I didn't do too bad with these which gave me hope my idea did have merit, and I highly recommend these for any would-be authors. But I didn't know much about marketing, so when I got online I decided to just be myself and try to make friends.

I also decided no more querying. I would self-publish. Soon I would give birth to my first daughter, my third and final child. Since I'd be at home for the years to come, I'd have the time to dedicate to making it happen, fail or succeed. My husband was on board, but at this point I'm sure it still seemed like a hobby to him. I think he would have done anything to lift my mood.

And then she was here. My darling baby girl. She is perfect and beautiful in every way. She's a sweet pinch of cinnamon, unlike her paler (but equally as cute) brothers.

As if by some miracle, all those dark thoughts left my world as she entered it. My anxiety was fading away. Pregnancy was over, birthing children was over. I could try to start over, too. It wouldn't be easy, but I would try.

*

It was April. The weather was turning, my body was no longer in constant agony. I could eat, drink, exercise, make love again. I felt grateful again. If I wasn't at home, could I write all my stories? If my husband wasn't so great, would I have the freedom to pursue this dream without constraint? I felt like my old self. Hating oneself is a burden no one should carry. It sucks.

So what does it take to self-publish? A lot of *ganas* (will) and balls.

I had previously researched the subject, but now I would have to become an expert, and start this whole author platform thing with a quickness. My paltry numbers on social media made me feel like a fly.

Here's a lesson: ignore the numbers and just be you. Social media is only one aspect of your platform and doesn't guarantee anything. Your own website is a great place to get started because it can serve as a platform for your creativity. I started with what I had and who I was for so many years. For all my wrongs and mistakes (lots of those), I think I have lived an interesting life.

Where I am today is miles away from where I started, even though I do feel like I'm right back there when pursuing new projects. The rejection won't stop, but if it is your passion you can overcome those feelings of self-doubt.

I also truly believe rejection is only as bad as you allow it to be. Yes, have a minute to stomp your foot, then crack on with the next submission.

Besides writing my own books, I also write reviews for a website (www.scifiandscary.com). I love film and wanted to showcase narratives from different countries. This evolved to books as I noticed there was a lack of diversity in books written by marginalized communities being reviewed.

Writing reviews has been a wonderful side project because I have met a fantastic team involved in the horror community. These like-minded individuals have made me feel less alone, both in life and on this writering journey. They have been there and done that.

We share our frustrations and joy. Same goes for the people I have met on Twitter and Instagram. You won't always agree with everyone on social media, however, you don't in day to day life either.

*

So that was my journey and no one else will walk the same path. Your journey is unique, embrace it even when it is hard – and there are times it *will* be hard. There are many things that could be perceived as obstacles and in some ways, they might be, however, I'm choosing to persevere and make them work.

I'm writing later in life. I'm a Mexican American woman. I write horror. I'm self published (as of now). I only write lead characters that are Latinx. The longer I do this, the more important it is for me to represent and lift up other marginalized voices. Even when I feel like giving up, I know I can't and shouldn't.

Neither should you.

My advice to writers:
- ✓ Write what is inside you.

  If you are a person from a marginalized group, write the story YOU want to tell and not the watered-down version you think others will like better. Only you can tell that story.
- ✓ It is never too late.

  I'm nearly forty and I feel I'm just getting started. To be honest, I don't think I could write my stories without the life experiences that have shaped me.
- ✓ Take your time and put on blinders.

  Social media can be a very useful tool, however, it can also flare self-doubt as you scroll through reading about all the things that seem to be happening to everyone but you. You can be that person good things happen to. Believe in yourself.
- ✓ Take social media breaks.

  If you feel yourself emotionally or mentally spiralling, just sign off for a bit. I have. There is nothing so very important that is worth your mental health. Focus on the writing.

- ✓ Be yourself.
  Don't feel you need to be the next J.K. Rowling or Stephen King. Why would you want to? It's been done.
- ✓ Be NICE!
  Get a bad review? Feeling hurt? Angry because you've poured every ounce of your time and soul in this project? It's ok to have those feelings, however, it is *not* ok to harass the person not enjoying your book. Will the reviewer turn around and say, "Hey, thanks for the abuse. I feel so different now. Best book ever!" Nope. Not going to happen. Just move on with the knowledge it is one opinion.
- ✓ Don't put down other books or authors.
  It's one thing to write a professional review stating a book wasn't your cup of tea, it is another thing to be personal or rude.
- ✓ Be your own biggest cheerleader, especially if you are a writer from a marginalized group.
  Our books and stories rarely get the spotlight, so tell people why what you have to say is important. Let them know you are there and want to be seen and heard.

My advice for Self Publishing:
- ✓ Be prepared to work your ass off with every aspect of publishing.
- ✓ GET AN EDITOR!
  If you can afford it, get someone to copy edit your work at the very least. I made the HUGE mistake of paying for an editor, and then changed things between the edit and publication that caused more errors. Make sure you check the manuscript again, and are happy with the finished product before you send it out.
- ✓ Invest in a cover.
  Whatever you can afford, go for it. This is the first thing people see, entice them into your world. You're the publisher, so this is your responsibility.
- ✓ Your book is a product so treat it as one.
  Be professional and considerate to everyone. If the waitress said, "Well, that is a shitty choice on the menu," followed by tossing your plate on the table, would you go back to that restaurant? Nope. A little customer service goes a long way.

✓ Submit your short stories.
You will get rejections, but short stories are useful for getting your name out there. They also helps hone your craft. Personally, writing short fiction is an outlet for me..

*

V. Castro is a Mexican American writer born and raised in San Antonio, Texas, and currently living with her family in London, UK. She is the author of Maria, The Wanted and the Legacy of The Keepers, *a vampire novel, and* The Erotic Modern Life of Malinalli The Vampire, *an erotic novella. Violet regularly contributes reviews, articles and stories to various horror websites. Follow her at www.vvcastro.com*

[Note: Portions of this essay first appeared in a different form as blog entries on V. Castro's Vampire Book Blog.*]*

Never Let Go
Wulf Moon

Barnacle glue, or barnacle cement, is one of the strongest adhesives known to man. Its tensile strength is 5000 pounds per square inch. It bonds so strong to boat hulls that after you shear the barnacle off, you're still going to have to grind away it's cement to be rid of it. A barnacle NEVER lets go.

Nor does a professional writer. You're reading this book, so there must be questions like this on your mind: Why does one writer become a pro writer, and another does not? Why does one writer talk about writing year after year, and yet another sees their work professionally published regularly?

I'll tell you why. It's because one writer never truly attaches to their dream of becoming a professional writer, while the other writer grabs onto the dream and never lets go.

In barnacles, the first stage, called the nauplius, is where the larvae mature as part of ocean plankton. It hasn't fully developed at this point, so it floats wherever the wind, waves, and tides may take it. Just like the barnacle, every single writer in existence has had their larval stage.

Aspiring writers get tossed about in their own larval stage, swept up in currents of conflicting misinformation, often generated by writing teachers and professors who mean well, but have no professional credits to their name. Worse, larval writers may be devoured by predators – editors and agents and contests that charge exorbitant fees with the promise of promoting or publishing their work, but in truth are just there to fleece desperate writers trying to navigate the overwhelming currents that seem to keep them from their destiny.

There's also storms and rocks that can not only take an aspiring writer off course, they can dash writing time to bits as writers fight real life battles to survive such things as job loss, severe health dilemmas, relationship issues, childcare – the list goes on and on.

And finally, there is perhaps the toughest battle of all – wrestling with our inner self. Are we worthy? Do we have what it takes? Will our writing efforts ever pan out? Will we even get to that successful sale and enjoy that glorious dawn of self-fulfillment as we see our work published and shared with the world?

The difference between storm-tossed plankton and the resolute barnacle is that one kept floating about the currents, while the other vigorously sought the next level of its existence – attaching to something solid and never letting go. The difference between a break-out writer and the novice is the same. If we wish to become a professional writer, we must keep seeking that goal. We must find a way to lock onto it and never let go.

The theme of this book is *How I Got Published and Never Let Go.*

Wait a minute. That's not quite right. It's *How I Got Published and What I Learned Along the Way.*

But my story of how I got published, of how I *continued* to get published, and what I learned along the way is indeed a tale of *never letting go...*

Call me Moon. I've been writing for over forty years.

*

My first professional sale came as the result of a writing contest. When I was fifteen, I won the national Scholastic Art & Writing Awards – the same contest that first discovered Stephen King, Peter S. Beagle, Truman Capote, John Updike, Joyce Carol Oates, and a host of iconic names in the arts. The editor at *Science World* saw my winning entry and bought and published my science fiction story in 1978. With professional pay and a circulation of 500,000 copies per issue, this was my first pro sale.

So here is the first lesson I learned, and I learned it young. **Amateur contests are an excellent way to get published.** How so? You're competing on a leveled playing field. When you submit to pro magazines, you are not. Competition is extremely tough there, because your story is up against stories written by seasoned veterans, many of them with tremendous skill and the prestigious awards to prove it! It should be a no-brainer that professional magazines are going to be hard to sell to at first, while winning contests that restrict entries to amateur writers is going to be easier.

Plus, winning a contest is a great ego boost, and in that battle against self-doubt – our worst enemy – having acknowledgment from a respected contest judged by bestselling professionals can help cement our belief that we can indeed become professional writers. In the case of the winners of Scholastic's contest, it's been said that these writers – by winning this national contest in their developmental stage – got an injection of proof that they could make a successful career in writing, and went into the world and made their belief reality.

Belief is a powerful thing. We must believe before we can accomplish. *Fake it till you make it* is a common phrase. But belief is something you don't fake. It's a fire in your gut you can't put out. You know you can do it; you just haven't had the full opportunity to prove it yet.

When George Mallory was asked by a newspaper reporter "Why did you want to climb Mount Everest?" he replied, "Because it's there." But I believe the true answer is, *"Because I knew I could."* He had climbed and trained on many mountains before he climbed Mt. Everest. He had proof positive he could do this thing. He had reached the pinnacle of other summits successfully. With that proof, he had the confidence to take on greater challenges. Winning writing contests will help you believe in your abilities, and with that proof, you can more easily forge ahead toward higher peaks in publishing.

Contests can also provide an aspiring writer with credits for cover letters, especially if they're respected for helping writers, not fleecing writers with expensive fees. I've won many such contests, including one sponsored by bestselling author Nora Roberts, where I won first place and got to write the conclusion to one of her novellas. I'm a professionally published Star Trek author now because I entered Pocket Books *Strange New Worlds* contest for new writers and was a winner in Volume 2. You think things like that look good on the cover letter you send with your story? You bet! They can act like a Sherpa to guide you straight out of the slush and onto those paths that lead right up to the editor-in-chief.

Want me to recommend a contest? I've got one for you. *Writers of the Future.* It's a speculative fiction contest, so if you write science fiction, fantasy, and soft horror, this contest is for you! This contest has been around for thirty-five years, there is no fee to enter, the judging is by some of the biggest bestselling writers in the industry, and it's restricted to amateur writers. If you have no more than three professional sales, you can enter this contest.

Don't get me wrong, there is serious competition, as thousands from around the world enter every quarter trying to win. But the benefits to a new writer make this the number one market you should be submitting to. Winners receive substantial prize and publication money, massive media promotion, and their stories get published in an international bestselling anthology.

There are many other benefits even if you don't win the contest. Setting a goal of entering every quarter teaches you how to meet a deadline. And as your writing rises toward professional standards, you will receive honor certificates that let you know how close your writing is to the professional mark. Semifinalists get comments on their story from the coordinating judge – this is a personalized critique from a *New York Times* bestselling author. Their quarterly deadlines also help you create new stories – and even if they don't win, you'll have more stories to send to other markets. I've sold several stories I wrote for this contest to professionally paying markets, and two have been reprinted – one in a best of the year anthology.

On top of that, there's the Writers of the Future Forum, an online forum where novice writers gather to discuss tips to help win the contest and to write professionally. It's a social forum where writers swap stories, share resources, and encourage one another to fuse themselves to their dream and never let go. I have a blog within that forum called Moon's SUPER SECRET Bonus Challenge. I set up the challenge because I'd noticed that a lot of novice writers rewrite and rework the same story over and over again, thinking they will perfect it. In truth, they often ruin it. So I established a challenge to get members to write and submit four fresh, original stories in a year. I also post writing tips and exercises, writing resources, and books to help aspiring writers create professionally crafted stories.

It must be working. Several of the forum members that have taken my challenge have become finalists in the contest since joining. Many members have written to me personally telling me my posts have helped them take up writing again. My SUPER SECRET topic has logged around 40,000 views, so I'm happy this resource has reached so many.

And this is my tip to you: *Come join us.* The people in this forum are helping one another navigate the currents so they can latch onto their dream of becoming professional writers. I have watched *many* of the members reach that goal over the years, including myself. (http://forum.writersofthefuture.com/)

*

I'm going to let you in on another secret, and *no one* is going to tell you this. I've had professional writers tell me to only send stories to professionally accredited markets, such as those approved by organizations like the Science Fiction and Fantasy Writers of America or the like. Start at the top paying markets on their list, stop at the lowest paying market still vetted by them as a professional sale. On the surface, this sounds logical. Who doesn't want the most money for their work, with the highest readership to broadcast their story out to? But for new writers, there can be a pitfall here. I'll give you my advice, since I'm supposed to be telling you What *I* Learned Along the Way.

Here's the deal. Professional 'zines need well-known authors to help sell their 'zines. When they publish a new, unheard-of author, do you see their name as a headliner? No. Why not? Because novice writers' names don't sell magazines. They have no following so it's pretty unlikely the publisher will put them on the cover (Caveat: *Future SF Digest* puts *every* author's name on the cover, bless this 'zine I work for.)

Editors *have* to buy good stories from well-known writers to sell their 'zines and stay in business. They love discovering new writers, don't get me wrong, but it's a business, and they need to sell copies to stay in business. There are very few openings in 'zines and professional anthologies for novice writers, and you are always competing against writers that have a good track record and proven professional skills. This is why it is difficult for new writers to break in.

Does this mean you should surrender, crawl away from the battle and send your writing to token or no pay markets instead? Not if your goal is to become a professionally published writer! I do not believe a writer should sell themselves short, nor give hard work away – except for good causes, like charity anthologies. But I don't believe we should limit ourselves to SFWA qualified (or HWA, RWA, etc.) markets only, as if the gold standard is the only currency.

Silver pays the bills as well, and performing on some of those slightly lesser stages can be the gateway to the fancy uptown theaters. You build a good resumé, and you keep trading up if your Broadway auditions aren't panning out. Yes, you still go to those Broadway auditions, but you are not above acting in a play just around the corner. In fact, I believe the more you play on those stages *close* to Broadway, the more likely that famous Broadway director will pay attention when you try out for their next production.

I didn't always think this way.

I came from a famous writing workshop filled with Nebula and Hugo and World Fantasy and Stoker winners. Almost all of them established pro's, telling you to focus on sending your work to SFWA and HWA approved markets and the like, because you can build your career by selling to the big name magazines and winning prestigious awards. That message was right for *them*. I don't believe it's the right message for a new writer. This is because a novice writer is still learning their craft. Like a novice actor, it's going to be rough getting work if you decide the only place you're willing to audition is on a Broadway stage.

And I still hear this rhetoric today. When I tell SFWA members my work is dancing across these stages, some automatically respond: 'I don't submit to any markets that aren't pro. My work should be worthy of professional pay.' I have to bite my tongue, but still say: "They PAID me SFWA pro pay." It's not like my story is a busker holding out a cup on Skid Row. These are Off Broadway productions, just around the corner from Big Name Theater.

Truth is, I shopped many of these stories for years to every SFWA accredited pro market. I got back wonderful personal rejections, but rejections aren't sales. So, with my new "Off Broadway, just around the block" thinking, I decided to step my search down to the next tier – pro pay but *not* SFWA qualified. Guess what? These pro and semi-pro level magazines and anthologies are in no way slumming. They have famous authors in every issue – and would *New York Times* bestselling authors send their stories to markets they felt would detract from their sterling reputations? Truth is, it's a way for these name authors to net up more fans. And I don't mind netting up more of those fans myself.

Such "SFWA only" rhetoric can be damaging to new writers. I know it held me back; I have changed that thinking now. I know precisely when I did, and I had immediate results. Walk with me. We're only going back two years.

*

It was a dark and stormy night. After hundreds of rejections on my stories and about 17 years since my last sale, I said, "Why don't I lower the Submission Grinder search engine to pro paying markets, but *not* SFWA qualified?"

Lo and behold, the first name that popped up was an anthology called *Strange Beasties.* I had a story called, *Beast of the Month.* The publisher, Third Flatiron, had a long history of creating anthologies that garnered great reviews, they paid the professional rate, and I had the perfect story to match their theme.

Guess what? It sold.

Then, they hired me to narrate it for podcast. And then I used that podcast as my demo, submitted it and got approved as a narrator at Escape Artists, Apex Publications, and Gallery of Curiosities. GoC regularly calls on me to narrate for them – it's been a great paying job.

But wait! There's more!

Third Flatiron paid me so *Beast of the Month* could appear in their Best of the Year anthology as well. And then the editor bought my story *War Dog* for another anthology. And hired me to narrate it. And that story went on to win Critters Readers' Choice Award for *Best Science Fiction and Fantasy Short Story of 2018*. And then editor Alex Shvartsman of UFO Publishing fame heard some of these podcasts, and hired me to be his podcast director at the professional 'zine *Future Science Fiction Digest*. And now I'm published there as well.

All because I changed my thinking, sent a story to a respected mid-level publisher... and worked my way up. That decision to change my standards and submit to semi-pro publishers – paying pro rate or just under – changed *everything* for me. I've been able to pay my mortgage many times this year from sales like this.

And guess what? It just keeps going up.

Once you sell a story to an editor, they watch for your work for future issues and anthologies. You've broken the ice, and if you've acted in a professional manner and made a good impression, they enjoy welcoming you back to their stage. You can build a career with an editor that loves your work. And as your visibility grows, other professional editors take note. The next story you send them might get more than just a first pages glance. It might get you a sale, and on to that Broadway stage you go.

*

I know the startup is hard. It can take many years to get professionally published with little to nothing giving you signs along the way. That's because those early stories are where you apprentice, they're your practice sessions where you learn your craft. Some writers don't survive the process – they take the volume of rejections as proof that they cannot write. The truth is, virtually every famous writer you know had to pass through this trial by fire. Why should it be any different for you or me?

Here is where you have to be that barnacle, resolutely fused to your goal, allowing nothing to shear you away. I have seen those writers cling to their dream, holding on through thick and thin. I have seen them battling the elements and fighting their own self-doubt. But I have also seen their breakout moment. They go for years selling nothing and then, all of a sudden, they're selling everywhere. To pro markets, winning awards. I've been happy for them. I know they exerted themselves with Herculean effort to get there.

Still, it's only natural to wonder, "When will *my* breakout moment come?"

Well, it does come – and usually when you least expect it.

In my case, four great things happened in a two-week span in August of 2018:

1. I was awarded a scholarship to the Superstars Writing Seminar, the best writing conference I have ever attended.
2. I sold *War Dog* to the *Terra Tara Terror* anthology, and it went on to win that best short story of the year award.
3. I won the international SF talent search *Writers of the Future* with my story "Super-Duper Moongirl and the Amazing Moon Dawdler."
4. And Alex Shvartsman asked me to be an editor at a new professional magazine, *Future Science Fiction Digest.*

All in a two-week period! All because I started thinking outside the box.

I had my breakout moment. I metamorphosed from amateur to professional writer.

And it can come for you as well. But to get there, you can never stop writing fresh stories, never stop learning your craft, and never stop believing you are a writer.

You must cling to your dream to become a professional writer just like a barnacle...and *never* let go.

Lessons learned:
✓ Enter *reputable,* no fee amateur writing contests, like *Writers of the Future.*
✓ Subscribe to and read the publications of the markets you submit to.
✓ Take writing courses by masters of the craft, like David Farland and Kevin J. Andersen.
✓ Attend *professional* writing seminars where you can learn from real pros that know what they're doing, like the *Superstars Writing Seminar.*
✓ Stop reworking old stories, thinking you can make them better. Write fresh stories!

- ✓ Write full time. If you can't do that, schedule *fresh story writing time* (not writing chat, not rewriting, not editing) each day if possible. Set an achievable word count – 500 words a day is a good one! – and *stick to your goal.*
- ✓ Send out your stories. They will never get published if you don't send them out. When they come back – and they will – send them back out and write your next story.
- ✓ Establish a *friendly* and *positive* social media presence focused on your goal of professional writing.

*

Wulf Moon is an Olympic Peninsula award-winning writer and podcast director for Future Science Fiction Digest. *His stories have been published in* Science World, Star Trek: Strange New Worlds 2, Writers of the Future Vol. 35, Future Science Fiction Digest, *and* Deep Magic. *He has won over thirty awards in writing, including the Critters Annual Readers' Choice Award for Best Science Fiction and Fantasy Short Story of 2018, the international Writers of the Future Contest, and Nora Roberts' contest where he wrote the conclusion to her novella* Riley Slade's Return.

Follow him on Facebook and at www.driftweave.com.

My Someday has Arrived
R.C. Scandalis

During my third grade parent teacher conference, my teacher, Mr. King, told my mother I should be a writer someday. I agreed with him, and from then on I knew I'd be an author.

But if we aren't careful, what is important to us, but not urgent, simply does not get done. When my fiftieth birthday arrived and I had yet to get started, I had a serious case of the "Oh Shits!" and realized with much trepidation that "someday" had arrived. I immediately vowed that I would be published before turning fifty one.

This seemed perfectly rational to me at the time. All I'd have to do was write a book, find an agent who would then immediately send the manuscript out to editors who would then buy it and turn it and me into an overnight sensation. No problem!

I have a BA and a teaching credential. And while I had focused on language, it was French, not English. I've read Voltaire, Baudelaire, Sartre and all the French classics, but my exposure to the American classics and the mechanics of writing fiction, my chosen path, were slim to nil.

Realizing I needed to learn more about the craft, I attended a writing conference held by a local writer's group. (I use the term local loosely – this particular writer's group is an hour away from my home.) Statistically people always do better on their goals with support, so after the conference I decided to find a group. Not wanting to travel that far, I tried out three other groups that were closer to home. None of them were the right fit for me, however, and eventually I decided to make the hour drive each week to be in the group that hosted the conference.

I really like this group because it is very large, so each time I get the benefit of a different group of people critiquing my work. I also like the variety of genres within the group and the varying levels of experience. Going as part of my weekly routine, whether or not I have something to read, keeps my writing goals top of mind and hearing other writers' opinions of my work is very helpful. Having to critique the other authors is useful, too. It develops me as a writer as well.

I keep a notebook for the group with two sections. One section is for critiquing. The other section is for notes to help me become a better writer, such as, "all scenes must advance the story in some way."

Learning to write better is really the quickest way to publication. I have a friend who has published a number of pieces and is in an online writer's group. I believe finding your tribe is an important key to your success. Your friends and family love you, but let's face it, they don't understand the life of a writer unless they are writers themselves. Having people to relate to will definitely make life easier.

At the conference I realized that I really had a lot more to learn and that there are certain elements of style and tools of the trade that will make your writing stronger. One of the presenters, David Farland, was offering a week-long intensive writing workshop. I liked his presentation. He is a prolific writer in his own right and has taught several other famous authors, so I felt like this was a great place to start. I signed up for his class.

Most of the attendees had flown in for the workshop and were staying onsite. I was commuting in for the daily sessions and showing houses in the evening instead of writing. I failed to complete my first assignment and struggled through the entire class to keep up. Still, it was an incredible experience that I wouldn't hesitate to do again. Workshops and conferences can be tax-deductible, I've learned, when you create a company and treat your writing like a business. Imagine that, paying less taxes while flying off to wonderful destinations to write and learn more about the craft. Sounds like a win win to me!

While in Farland's course I made some great connections. One was with a woman, Chris Abela, who raved about Superstars, an annual conference that was different from the typical writer's con in that it was about the business of writing. Owning a real estate company myself, I immediately recognized the importance of understanding the business side of this creative endeavor. I signed up then packed up for Colorado.

Again I soaked up what I could and bought the audio files for what I couldn't. Things were covered that I had expected, like timelines, contracts and the editing process. But I learned other things I hadn't even thought about. For instance, I was adamant that I did not want to self-publish, but I learned that many authors these days do a combination. One reason is because the traditional route typically takes years, even for sequels, and readers want your next book NOW. So many authors self-publish in between releases from their publishing house. I kept an open mind, which allowed me to change it regarding self-publishing and now I expect to self-publish at some point in my career.

And yes, I said to be traditionally published takes *years*.

If that shocked you, well, it shocked me, too, to learn that it typically takes at least two years from completing your manuscript to publication – and that's not counting all the time it takes to find an agent and market your book to prospective publishers – assuming it is publishable at all. Talking to numerous authors this past year, one of the most common things I heard is that their first book, or two – or three! – were unpublishable.

It's funny that it never occurred to me that my first book might not ever get published. I am not sure why I expected the first thing I wrote to be a masterpiece, but I suspect this is common among us dreamers. We love our art, so naturally everyone will, right? We don't think about writing as a skill to develop, like playing an instrument. We would never expect a violinist, who also loves his art, to wake up one morning, pick up a bow and believe the world would love the sounds that emerge. Why then, do authors pick up a pen and expect to write a classic from word one? I was horrified to learn that would most likely not be the case.

While I understood the sense of it, this realization was a serious setback for my timeline. I'd need time to write lousy so I could get good. Then I'd need time to find an agent, who'd need time to find a publishing house. And once the publishing house picked up my book, they'd need a year or more to put it in print. My goal of being published within the year was not looking good. I had already established that self-publishing didn't count for my goal. But I was not willing to give up my dream of being published before my next birthday. There had to be another way!

It was then that I began writing short fiction and poetry. The criteria was simple: The project had to be something that touched, moved or inspired me.

So I created an email account specifically for my writing and a spreadsheet where I tracked where I sent my submissions and when I would hear back from each. I had to have something out at all times. Ideally I wanted to have multiple submissions out at once. All had some sort of prompt or theme, although there are plenty of editors accepting submissions without any parameters besides story length.

I wrote children's stories, science fiction, poetry and Americana. One project was to take a painting and write a story about it. One was a five line Haiku. Some submissions were to competitions that required an entrance fee. Some were free. Some had a quick response time some took several months. I subscribed to several writer websites and used online sources such as Submittable and Writer's Relief to find opportunities.

Many of the opportunities came directly from the different communities of writers I belong to. I also bought a subscription to *Writer's Digest* and looked in *Writer's Market*. Luck and grace played a huge part but I believe approaching my writing with intention and focus really paid off. Ten months into my fiftieth year, my poem *The Cellphone* was published in *Quoth the Raven*, an anthology of contemporary reimaginings of the works of Edgar Allen Poe.

As of this writing, I turn fifty-one in three weeks. Reflecting on this first year as a writer, I wish I could say that I wrote four hours every day, which was my goal setting out. I'd like to say I wrote two hours every day, but I didn't do that, either. But what I did do was stay the course. Some days I only wrote thirty minutes, some not at all, but my commitment to being a writer never wavered. I didn't get discouraged and I never gave up. I was kind to myself and gave myself encouragement. Instead of beating myself up for not writing, I drew strength and encouragement from the writing I had done.

I think associating being a writer with my identity also made a huge difference. I am a writer. It's who I am. If you're reading this, it's who you are, too. And it's important to get that. *You are a writer.* You don't need someone to publish you to make that true. I think once I understood that for myself I became more confident and began to take this endeavor more seriously.

This has been a wondrous year. I have learned much. Of course I have much left to learn. This year I plan to divide my time between writing for submissions and beginning that first, awful book. Who knows? Maybe I'll get lucky and it will be one of the unicorns that become a bestseller. But even if its utter rubbish, I am more interested in the process and can't wait to see where it takes me.

When I started out, I would get frustrated if I didn't feel every word was perfect as it hit the page. I know now that sometimes you have to keep writing, even if it doesn't feel like its flowing—and that most likely it won't really come together until the second or third draft. This knowledge is freeing.

What else will I learn over the course of writing a book? Of course I don't know yet. Some lessons we can't learn by reading about them, or listening to podcasts, both of which I have done lots of this year. We have to learn by doing. I know sticking with the same storyline for 50,000 words or more will teach me lessons I can't learn until I've done it. I'm ready! How about you?

What I learned:
- ✓ Have the right mindset. Think of yourself as a writer. Tell people you are a writer. You don't need to be published to be a writer. You need to write to be a writer.
- ✓ Create a goal for yourself and keep that goal in sight, even when you don't meet it. Don't give up! And don't beat yourself up for not meeting it. Congratulate yourself for the progress you have made as any progress is an accomplishment!
- ✓ Learn more about the craft. While you don't need a master's in creative writing, the more tools you have at your disposal, the better your writing will be.

- ✓ Network with other writers. Go to conferences. Join a writer's group. The more people that are involved with your dream, the better! They will help make it more real.
- ✓ Most writing requires several drafts. This is normal! It doesn't mean you are a bad writer, it means you are a typical writer.
- ✓ Keep a spreadsheet of your submissions so you know what you have out, where you have sent it and when you should hear back.

*

Renee Scandalis has a history in publishing dating back to her tenure as a junior high school teacher in Northern California, where she served both as editor and occasional guest contributor of the journalism club's monthly newspaper. She currently lives in the Dallas-Fort Worth area, where she runs a boutique real estate company, and is a member of the DFW Writer's Workshop. Her first professional publication was the poem, The Cellphone, *which was published in the Poe-themed anthology* Quoth the Raven *in 2018.*

Follow her at www.arceewrites.com

It Takes as Long as it Takes

A. Lee Martinez

It was a weird path.

I wasn't one of those kids who always dreamed of being a writer. I just fell into it, and like most things I fell into, it started with boredom.

If I'd been born later, with access to the internet and streaming media and a thousand and one distractions, I probably never would've become a writer. It's odd to think of it now, but in ye olde 80's, entertainment was scarce, and I didn't have many friends. So I spent my time at home, not doing much. It didn't help that I grew up in an unincorporated town without a mall or a movie theater or much of anything.

One summer, they opened a convenience store within walking distance, and my biggest treat was to walk the mile or so to buy a soda and play a couple of rounds of *Black Tiger*, an obscure video game that nobody else seems to remember but me.

I'd always drawn cartoons because notebooks were cheap and available, and it was easy to doodle in my spare time. There's only so much to be done with a notebook and a pen, so I started writing stories. It was mostly a hobby at that point.

The great thing about being a loner in school is that if you find a quiet corner to sit and draw and write in a notebook, most people will leave you alone. I was an awkward kid, so being left alone appealed to me. I whiled away my lunch break and free moments writing and drawing in notebooks, and this might have been the end of it if not for a couple of important people.

Mom always cultivated my artistic ambitions. It was her idea for me to write a story at first, and while that first effort didn't get far, springboarding off her inspiration led to me writing. I was never embarrassed or shamed for writing.

I had one particularly study hall where a teacher suggested I read instead of draw, and when he threatened to call Mom, I informed her with trepidation. She laughed it off.

Thanks, Mom. You're the best.

The other person who started me on this path was my English teacher, a lovely woman who I have long since forgotten the name of, much to my shame. It was she that suggested I enter a local short story contest, which I did. My story was a weird little tale of an alien pilot arguing with an artificially intelligent computer in an effort to save them both.

It won.

Now, I have no idea of the quality of the stories submitted. Heck, it's been so long, I barely remember my story at all, but I won the contest, and I thought this was a pretty cool thing, writing stories for money. Sure, this story only won me a $25 savings bond, but it was the beginning of bigger, brighter things.

Mom still has the savings bond, last time I checked. Even when things were getting dicey financially, she couldn't cash it. I'm surprised she hasn't framed it yet.

It was at that moment that I embarked on the journey to becoming a professional novelist. Thirteen short years later, it eventually happened. If I'd known it would've taken that long, I might not have even started. Which brings me to the most important thing I've learned from this journey:

It takes as long as it takes.

*

I know plenty of novelists now. Most found publication faster. Some didn't. But there is no universal time limit one can appeal to. Everyone writes at their own pace. Everyone edits at their own pace. The submission process can be long and painful or, if you're very lucky, short and sweet. The publication process is always longer than anyone expects. Sometimes, it's fast, but even fast, it's usually pretty slow. Each of us is not on someone else's pace. We're on our own, and that long and winding path is always going to take longer than you expect.

Independent press and self-publishing can be faster paths toward publication, but walk these at your peril, and beware anyone who promises to fast track your book to publication. Be suspicious of anyone who thinks publishing a solid book can be done in mere weeks.

Self-publishing becomes more viable with each passing year, but it's a heck of a lot of work to do right. Most people do not do it right, and it shows. There are no shortcuts to making a great book. Or even a merely good one.

I can't speak to the temptation to hastily self-publish because in my aspiring artist days vanity press existed, but it was hardly a path to larger success. It cost a significant amount of money, and in the end, you usually ended up with several dozen boxes of books nobody really wanted.

Things have changed. Now it's a heck of a lot cheaper, and instead of all those boxes, you can end up with an e-book buried beneath the ten zillion e-books published daily. I suppose that's progress.

*

None of this is meant to discourage you from seeking out your own path. I've been published for fifteen years now, and in that time I've gone from an unknown writer to a merely obscure one.

Another lesson: You've never "made" it. The path doesn't have an end. It just has the occasional nice scenic overlook.

For me, the first thirteen years were fairly barren. I wrote. I polished. I submitted. In return, I was greeted with mostly yawning indifference from the publishing world. Every so often, I'd get something other than a form rejection. Rejections still, mind you, but a *personalized* rejection can be like an oasis through that desert.

I recall an editor actually calling me in person to tell me they liked my novel, but that they couldn't sell it to the editors-in-chief. It was a wonderful high to be rejected but told to keep writing.

You take what you can get on the path.

I ended up at a larger publisher by happenstance. He was taking over his position at Tor Publishing and kept meeting members of my writers group at different writing conferences. After the third or fourth person mentioned my name to him, he sent word that I submit to him.

At the time, it was just another potential rejection. I'd been working at it for years and with not much to show for it but a pile of manuscripts that were getting good feedback, but not inspiring anyone to accept them. I was pretty low at that point. I didn't regret the time I'd put into writing, but there's a time when you have to consider moving on. I was considering.

Then came the acceptance.

I'd like to say that it was a moment of awesome, but by then, I was burnt out. It wasn't that I wasn't excited. I was, very much so. But all my energy had been spent getting here, and enthusiasm was hard to come by.

There's a lot to the publishing process. Contracts to be signed, edits to be made, waiting for publication. It's a process that takes as long as it takes, and by the time my first book hit the shelves, I was hopeful.

I was lucky with that first book. It garnered more attention than the average first book, and buoyed by that success, I managed to eventually land a movie option. It takes a while for a studio to develop a movie, and most options don't go anywhere. Mine ultimately didn't, though it did lead some terrific opportunities working on a few other potential movie projects that didn't go anywhere either.

I don't say this as a negative because it was all a great experience, and I was paid for my work. Getting paid is always nice, and I worked with some great people, but I never thought of myself as anything other than a novelist. I was still writing my books.

*

The next lesson: Keep writing. If you're a writer, you write. That's your job. Even if you're not being paid for it, if you want to eventually get paid for it, you have to write. There's no end goal that takes you beyond writing. Writing is what you do.

That never stops being the goal. The other stuff that you hope comes with it, getting your book or script or poem or what-have-you into the public eye, of perhaps getting paid for it, or perhaps getting a significant amount of people excited about it, those are all wonderful possibilities. But if you view writing as a means to an end, you probably won't make it far in this business. Which brings me to my final lesson:

There is a difference between writing for fun and writing to be a professional.

If you want to write for fun or as a hobby, I say go for it. As an art form, it's hard to beat. You just need some paper and a writing implement. Heck, almost all of us have this word processing box in our house that we already have sitting there doing other stuff for us, so it's not as if there's a great expense. And while writing well is not easy, pursuing your own interest in writing is as simple as plopping down in your favorite chair and scribbling down words with the intent of scribbling out words better each day.

But if you're interested in being a professional, in getting actual money for what you write, then you have to approach it as you would any other job, except this job doesn't have a boss looking over your shoulder or annual employee assessments. When you first start writing, no one is going to fire you if you don't write. The opposite will often be true. There will be obstacles on the path. You will struggle to find time. Every time your writing improves, you'll be reminded of how far you've come, but also how far you have to go. You will be discouraged. You will fail.

You will fail a lot.

That's the path of professional aspiration, and it isn't an easy one, and while it isn't always obstacles, the moments of reward are rare. But when they come, they can be so very sweet. If you are persistent enough to weather the storm to reach them.

So write. Polish. Submit. Never stop improving. Never take rejection personally. Savor every victory.

But, above all, keep writing.

Lessons learned
- ✓   It takes as long as it takes. There are no shortcuts.
- ✓   Everyone has their own path to publication.
- ✓   Finish your project. An unfinished project does no one any good, especially you.

- ✓ Strive to improve. Your writing can always be better.
- ✓ Submit. You can only polish so much. The worst finished novel beats the best unfinished novel every time.

*

A. Lee Martinez has written 12 science fiction / fantasy novels. His novels have received a Best Books for Young Adults award, an Alex Award, and The Amelia Bloomer Award. His debut novel, Gil's All Fright Diner, *and fourth novel,* The Automatic Detective, *received starred reviews in* Publisher's Weekly. *In his spare time he enjoys playing tabletop games and watching monster movies. He lives outside of Dallas with his wife and too many pets accumulated by two people who should really know better.*

Going Pro
David Farland

It seems that every writer breaks into his or her career using a different path. You find a door into publishing, and as soon as you get through, the door disappears behind you. I've known authors who have broken in the traditional way, by sending manuscripts to agents. I've known others who went directly to the editors to submit. I've seen people self-publish their own books and make millions, and I've watched novelists move into the field from writing for games or screenplays. In short, there are a million ways to start a writing career.

I took an unusual path.

When I was in college studying to be a doctor, I had hoped to "write on the side." But the urge became too strong and I decided to work toward making a living at it. In looking at the possible majors that might help me become a writer, I wasn't pleased with "English" as a major. However, I heard about a program at the university that would allow me to tailor my own major to suit my career goals. So I created a "writing and editing" major, where I combined writing, editing, and the study of modern literature in such a way that I felt I would be a good fit to get hired by a major publisher while I worked toward writing as a career.

I think that this helped a lot.

I know that the university loved it: they used my program as a template to create their own English writing and editing tracks, and the program was so popular that 180 other colleges created similar programs over the next 10 years.

In fact, while I was still in school, I was hired by the college to help edit papers by professors who were seeking publication. This was the highest-paying job offered to undergrads, and of course the job led to better offers elsewhere.

Lesson learned: **Blaze your own path to success no matter how crazy it might seem to others.**

But let's stick to writing fiction. While I was an undergrad, after I turned in my first short story to a creative writing teacher, she suggested that I should submit it for an upcoming writing contest. I dusted it off and dropped it into the submissions box. A few weeks later, I won third place in the contest.

Lesson learned: **Take your chances and begin submitting early.**

The check was small – only $50 – but when I did the math, I realized that I had made $7 per hour while writing that short story, which was more than double the minimum hourly wage at that time. I wondered if by spending more time on writing, I might have been able to win the $500 dollar prize. So I set a goal: for the next year, I wanted to win that prize.

Lesson learned: **Aim higher.**

I made a list of upcoming contests and began to figure out how to win them. As much as possible, I did some detective work and found out who the judges were going to be. I then read works by the prospective judges and tried to figure out what their own personal values were in literature. How old were the protagonists in their stories? What sex were they? Did they prefer humor or romance to drama? Were there particular themes that cropped up in their works? What types of hooks and metaphors did they employ? Did they prefer lyrical storytelling to plain tales?

Lesson learned: **Research your markets, whether they be editors, agents, contest judges, critics, or just plain readers.**

Once I had some direction, I wrote my heart out. I soon realized that I couldn't always know who my editors or agents might be, and so I had to come up with ways to please everyone. Now, that might not seem possible, but once again, I got to thinking. I asked myself, on a scale of 1-10, how good is my characterization? How good is my plot? How great is my pacing? How strong are my metaphors? How well does my opening hook readers? Does my story have the intellectual depth and resonance I'm seeking? How powerfully pleasing is the end? I made up a list of about 40 ways that I wanted my story to be excellent, and then I worked at writing a story that hit tens across the board.

My theory was that I couldn't know who my competition was, and so I had to plan on being beaten in one or two categories, so I wanted to be excellent in every way that I could imagine.

Lesson learned: Struggle for excellence.
No one wants your second-best effort.

So I composed a story and tried to make it error-free. I didn't want any typos or dropped words to distract from my presentation. I wanted the work to look professional. And I got to thinking about subtle things.

For example, at the time, submissions were going in on paper, and I got to thinking: If I used a 20-pound bond paper, wouldn't my submission feel somehow weightier, more substantial, to the judges? And what about my font choice? Does it scream, "This should be in a major magazine?"

So I went to the trouble of putting my story on bond paper and even put a dab of cologne on the last page of the manuscript so that it would infuse the manuscript with a pleasant scent, then stuck it in an envelope so that it would be ready for the upcoming contest.

Lesson learned: Don't wait for the last minute to make a
great impression.

When I was done, I had a good six months before the contest would even open, and I realized that I had time to write a story for a second contest, and a third and a fourth and a fifth and sixth. So I repeated the process with other contests.

Lesson learned: Don't just take one shot. Keep shooting
until the barrel of your revolver starts to melt.

The deadlines for the contests came and went, and I submitted my stories, hoping to win first place in one. I soon got a call: I'd won first place in that little contest that I'd first hoped to win – a prize of $500. Two days later, I won first place in another contest, this time for a thousand dollars. Then I won first place in a third contest – a small one that only paid $100. About two weeks after winning that first prize, I found that I had won the first place in the *L. Ron Hubbard Writers of the Future Contest*, a large international contest that not only paid $1000 for first place, but also paid another $1000 for publication and had a grand prize of $5000 more. The contest was also going to fly me to New York for a big writing workshop.

Lesson learned: **There are opportunities all around you. Grab onto them before they go away.**

As I considered this last contest, I could see that it would lead to bigger things. I'd hoped to become a published author someday, well after I graduated from college, but realized that in the meantime I was going to have to get to work. Shortly after this, I got hired to help professors at Brigham Young University get their works published, so between school, a career, and being a new dad I didn't have time to push my own writing.

Lesson learned: **Make time to succeed. You'll never "find the time," you have to *make* it.**

I decided to outline a book based upon my prize-winning story, and soon began to have very strange dreams set in the world of my science fiction novel. Now, I was writing a mainstream novel at the time, but I decided to abandon it.

Lesson learned: **Follow your dreams. That is how your subconscious speaks to you – in dreams.**

About a month before the big awards ceremony, I heard a rumor that two of the judges from the contest were going to gang up on me and see if they could get a novel contract out of me. Knowing that probably wasn't helpful – I got too excited, and I don't think I got much done for several weeks.

Lesson learned: **Dream big but don't get too excited. Far too often reality will slap you in the face.**

I went to the workshop and had a great time, and I did win the grand prize for the year. It would have been fun to take the $5000 and go on a honeymoon with my wife, but instead I used most of it to buy a new computer and invest in my career.

Lesson learned: **Keep writing income sacred. Invest in yourself.**

At the awards ceremony atop the World Trade Center, I was approached by eight different editors who gave me their cards and asked that I submit a novel proposal. I noticed that two or three of them offered their cards with shaking hands, and I realized that they were more nervous than I was.

Lesson learned: **Remember that publishers and readers are aching to find good new writers.**

I had come prepared for just such an occasion. I'd brought three copies of my novel proposal, but wasn't sure which editor to choose.

Lesson learned: **Consciously choose who to submit to. Don't just pick an editor or agent because they would be happy to have you.**

So I went home and researched agents. I wanted one with a powerful client list, someone who could help me make a career out of this. I also wanted someone who had a few lesser-known writers as clients. In other words, I wanted someone who might be willing to take a chance on me, a new writer. I called her on the phone and explained my situation.

She said, "Well, I haven't taken on a new client in eight years, but one of my writers just committed suicide last night, so I'll take you."

Lesson learned: **Don't be afraid to cold-call a big agent, editor, or movie producer. We're all in the same business.**

I felt worried that I didn't have a huge publishing portfolio, but my agent said, "That's all right. Publishers are just looking for authors who are 'proven' authors. By winning all of these writing contests, you have become a proven author." I learned that you can become a proven author by winning awards, publishing short stories in several markets, or by publishing novels with others.

Lesson learned: **Every new author feels "imposter syndrome." Don't give into it. A new writer is still a *real* writer.**

I faxed my novel proposal to my new agent the next morning. By three in the afternoon she called with offers from three of the publishers that had approached me. They were all pretty good offers, and we discussed the merits of each publisher.

One publisher, Bantam Books, was huge in the science fiction market at the time, and had an advantage: they spent more money on marketing their books than the other publishers did, so my agent felt that they sold nearly twice as many copies as any of the other publishers.

They weren't offering as high a royalty rate as one of the competitors, but my agent felt we would make up for it in sales. I told my agent that I wanted that higher royalty rate as well, so she negotiated the royalty rate up.

Lesson learned: **All publishers are not equal. Look for the one who makes the most money in your genre and you'll typically find a publisher who invests heavily into the genre and knows how to make a sale.**

Now the real work began. I had to write a danged novel, and I'd never done it before. So I just sat down and went to work on it. I was very ill at the time with chronic fatigue syndrome, so it turned into an arduous task. I had to quit my job and drop out of school as a senior, but I found that as long as I focused my creative energy on writing, the words flowed pretty well.

I had set a number of writing goals for my book. I wanted it to be seen as "deep" and "powerful" so as I wrote each scene, I did it to the best of my ability. I even wrote down a list of "goals" for my novel, ways that I hoped to excel. I just followed my instincts and tried to make each scene engrossing to me, rather than worry about what anyone else might think.

When I finished, I turned it in to my agent. She wrote, "For a guppy, you sure swim in deep waters!"

Lesson learned: **Write a review for your novel before you begin so that you are clear as to what it is that you hope to accomplish.**

When I turned the book in to my editor, I felt very concerned by one chapter. I had my protagonist have a long philosophical discussion late into the night.

My protagonist was a doctor, a mercenary on a ship with thousands of other mercenaries flying to a foreign war being waged between two Japanese corporations on a distant planet. He spoke with a general about all kinds of topics – the nature of good and evil, and what it was they were hoping to accomplish. .

I wanted to recreate those rambling conversations that I sometimes had with good friends, but I worried that the scene was too odd.

The first draft of the chapter was more than 130 pages long. So I asked my editor to let me know what I should cut. She called me up the following week and said that not only had she read it, but also her boss, the head of the publishing company. She said that she wanted me to add 10,000 words.

I explained to her that I couldn't add anymore. I did what I called "syllabic editing," where I had cut every single extraneous syllable that I could see in the story, and I really couldn't see anything to add. She said, "What we want is a 10,000-word essay where you tell us how in the hell a new writer like you was able to write such a book. This is amazing!"

Lesson learned: **A wizard never writes a book
that is too long or too short.
Every book must be just the right length.**

Overall my editor was very happy. There were only a few typos in the book, but my editor did have one question:

"On page 186, what in the hell is Abriara Cifuentes wearing?"

To be honest, I'd never thought about that. My answer was kind of lame: "Clothes."

So she ordered me to spend a page "dressing" my character.

Lesson learned: **Every writer has a few blind spots.
Some don't add background like mountains and stars.
Others never think about their character's**

day jobs or medical history.
Find out what your blind spots are and address them.

When the reviews started to come in, I was very happy. *Publishers Weekly* called it a "deep" novel and said that "by keeping his moral vision firmly wedded to a compelling plot, Wolverton creates a novel with powerful emotional resonance."

The Magazine of Fantasy and Science Fiction called it "One of the deepest and most powerful science fiction novels ever written," and said that "many fine novels that have won Hugos and Nebulas pale in comparison."

So when the book came out and debuted at #2 on the science fiction bestseller lists, I felt really surprised. My books debuted higher than those written by several of my heroes.

Lesson learned: **People love new authors and are**
always looking for someone to discover.
Critics can be your best advertisers.

The book went on to win the Philip K. Dick Memorial Special Award as one of the best novels of the year. It remained on the bestseller list for five months, and while the little advance that I'd gotten was great, I made a lot more in royalties. The book went on to sell for years, was translated into foreign languages, and still makes me money online. It won an award in Canada for being the most checked-out book in their library system for the year, and at a convention in Russia it placed #2 as the all-time best book ever written in science fiction.

Lesson learned: **Your book takes on a life of its own.**
You never know where and when it might succeed.
Think of it as a long-term investment that could pay
great dividends from any country in the world.

The success of my first novel served as a stepping stone. My second novel debuted at #1 on the science fiction bestseller list because I had built up an audience that recognized my name and was hungry for my work.

I soon learned that, as an author, people come to expect more from you – more books – and they want more and more from you.

They want your next book and they want it to be better than the last one that you wrote.

Lesson learned: **Your goal as a writer is to oblige the reader. With each novel that you write, search for some way to make it *better* than the last.**
If readers feel that each book is *worse* than your others, they will abandon you as an author.

Over the past thirty years I've helped hundreds of writers achieve their first publication. Nearly a hundred of my writing students have gone on to become New York Times bestselling writers, and several of them have become #1 New York Times bestsellers.

I think that the reason I've been able to help so many of them is that I struggle to teach them not just how to write beautifully, but also how to get on a successful career track. In other words, as new writers, I want to see my students learn not only how to write, but how to manage the business aspects of writing.

This means that I need to teach my students how to sell a novel, how to deal with editors and contracts, how to keep inspired and creatively exciting.

Lesson learned: **Having a successful career requires more than just writing.**

Here's to your success!

Lessons learned:
- ✓ Blaze your own path to success no matter how crazy it might seem to others.
- ✓ Take your chances and begin submitting early.
- ✓ Aim higher.
- ✓ Research your markets.
- ✓ Struggle for excellence. No one wants your second-best effort.
- ✓ Don't wait for the last minute to make a great impression.
- ✓ Don't just take one shot.
- ✓ There are opportunities all around you. Grab onto them before they go away.
- ✓ Make time to succeed. You'll never "find the time," you have to make it.

- ✓ Follow your dreams. Dream big but don't get too excited.
- ✓ Keep writing income sacred. Invest in yourself.
- ✓ Remember that publishers and readers are aching to find good new writers.
- ✓ Consciously choose who to submit to.
- ✓ Don't be afraid to cold-call a big agent, editor, or movie producer.
- ✓ Every new author feels "imposter syndrome." Don't give into it.
- ✓ All publishers are not equal.
- ✓ Write a review for your novel before you begin so that you are clear as to what it is that you hope to accomplish.
- ✓ A wizard never writes a book that is too long or too short.
- ✓ Every writer has a few blind spots. Find out what your blind spots are and address them.
- ✓ People love new authors and are always looking for someone to discover. Critics can be your best advertisers.
- ✓ Your book takes on a life of its own. You never know where and when it might succeed.
- ✓ Your goal as a writer is to oblige the reader.
- ✓ Having a successful career requires more than just writing.

*

Dave Wolverton writes fantasy under the name of David Farland. He is a New York Times bestseller with over sixty books and novels in print and has helped dozens of other writers become bestsellers, too. His past students include Brandon Sanderson (Way of Kings), Brandon Mull (Fablehaven), Stephenie Meyer (Twilight), James Dashner (The Maze Runner), and many more. He is the lead judge for the world's largest science fiction and fantasy writing contest. Dave also teaches writing workshops, writes screenplays, and designs videogames. You can find out more about his books and workshops at www.mystorydoctor.com

About the Editor

Lyn Worthen has been reading since before she can remember, and began her career as a freelance writer and editor sometime in the previous century. And while non-fiction paid the bills for many years, her love for the written word ultimately led her back to fiction. Lyn currently serves as Managing Editor at Camden Park Press, and divides her time between building award-winning short fiction anthologies, and editing for indie fiction authors. In her spare time, she also writes fiction in multiple genres under various pen names.

For more information about other Camden Park Press anthologies, visit *www.camdenparkpress.com*

For more information about indie editing services, visit *www.camdenparkediting.com*

About BundleRabbit

BundleRabbit is the premier DIY book bundling service. We help readers save money on ebooks by providing authors with the tools to bundle their books together and offer them at a discount.

BundleRabbit also provides an amazing service for multi-author projects: Collaborative Publishing. With collaborative publishing, co-author or multi-author projects can be created and published in both ebook and print formats and distributed through the major online retailers without the individual authors having to deal with the headache of tracking and splitting royalties among all participants.

Visit *BundleRabbit.com* to discover more.

Other Anthologies from Camden Park Press

Mirages and Speculations

Science fiction and fantasy stories
from the desert.
A Critters' Reader's Poll "Top Ten" selection

www.books2read.com/Mirages

Quoth the Raven

Contemporary reimaginings
of the work of Edgar Allan Poe.
Bram Stoker Award nominee *(preliminary ballot)*
Winner of the Critters' Reader's Poll
"Best Anthology" award

www.books2read.com/QuothTheRaven

Wings of Change

Stories about dragons and the
young people whose lives they change.

www.books2read.com/WingsOfChange

Love Among the Thorns

Contemporary Gothic/Paranormal romance.

www.books2read.com/Thorns

Available October 30, 2019